STAIN TYPES

The three main stain types are:

Protein stains
Tannin (wet) stains
Greasy (dry) stains

The importance of identifying the type of stain you are dealing with cannot be overstated. Your instincts may be to reach for the hot-water tap or a bar of soap and scrub away, but if you are using the wrong method for that particular stain, you could easily be setting the stain permanently into the fabric.

The don'ts in this book are, therefore, as crucial as the dos. The two most important of these, which should ensure you never have a stain disaster again, are:

DON'T use hot water or heat on protein stains, as this will set many of these stains permanently.
DON'T use any kind of soap on tannin stains, as this will set many of these permanently.

Identifying protein stains

You can tell a protein stain by its source: if organic, it's likely to be protein. Many basic food stains, such as egg, milk, yogurt and cheese sauce, come from animal products and so are protein stains. All stains resulting from the bodily functions of humans and animals – such as blood, urine and vomit – are protein, as are those that come from the earth, like mud. Grass is protein, but is classified as special because it is more difficult to remove.

Some food stains, such as gravy, chocolate and tomato sauce, are protein/grease combination stains. Always treat the protein part first – that is, use cold water, then go on to treat the grease part of the stain.

Tip
Beware of unknown red stains.
If they could possibly be blood that's not yours, wear protective rubber gloves.

Protein stains

Removal rating: Easy
These are the easiest stains to remove, provided you don't use any kind of heat, and can usually be removed completely by rinsing in cold water, followed by a cool biological (enzyme) soak if necessary.

Biological detergents and pre-soak products usually contain several kinds of enzymes, because different proteins respond to different enzymes. Potatoes are natural enzyme 'stain sticks' – slice a potato in half and rub it over any dried-in stain for a few minutes before laundering. They are also useful as a quick spot dirt remover on non-washable (dry-clean only) fabrics.

Tannin (wet) stains

Removal rating: Moderate
To identify a tannin stain, ask yourself if it comes from a wet, liquid source or a dry, greasy source. Tannin stains are direct liquid spills from alcohol, perfumes, inks, melted ice lollies, fruit juices, tea and coffee. They respond well to hot water, but will set permanently if you use any kind of soap. Apart from sugar tannin stains (see below), you can launder these stains with detergent in the hottest water that is safe for the fabric.

A quick treatment for fresh tannin stains is to suspend the fabric, stain side down, over a bowl and secure with a rubber band or clothes pegs. Pour on hot water from as great a height as possible without danger of splashing. The force will rinse through the fabric, taking the stain with it. Use an acid stain stick on old, stubborn stains (see page 17).

Sugar tannin stains

These include alcohol, cakes, soft drinks, ice lollies and non-dye ice pops, and are combination protein/tannin stains that should be rinsed in cold water, or soda water if you have it. If treated immediately, they are easy to remove. Older stains should be soaked in a biological (enzyme) detergent. If this doesn't work, bleaching may be the only solution.

Point out sugar stains on non-washable fabrics to the dry cleaner, as they may have dried into the fabric and become invisible. In time they will caramelize, turn brown and be impossible to remove. For immediate spills on non-washables, mix white vinegar with water in equal parts, spot on and rinse off.

Greasy (dry) stains

Removal rating: Moderate
Greasy stains result from any product containing fat or oil and respond well to hot water and detergent. Never iron a fabric with any trace of grease – heat will set the stain.

Washing-up liquid is manufactured to remove grease from crockery and it also works well on fabric. Often, all you need to do is apply a little neat non-gel washing-up liquid to both sides of the stain and agitate the back of fabric against itself under the hot tap. Apply a little more washing-up liquid and leave on while you launder as usual.

Do not leave greasy clothes soaking in detergent and water that has gone cold. The grease particles will break down but will then redistribute themselves throughout the fabric, making it dirtier than it was before. Grease stains on nylon and man-made fibres can be difficult to remove if left for more than a day.

Treat old, stubborn stains with a grease-solvent stain remover, but never use solvents on highly inflammable petrol or diesel stains. If you do not have a solvent, apply a paste of detergent powder and water, then launder in the hottest water safe for the fabric. Spot treat non-washables with dry-cleaning spot remover.

Other stains

To the three main categories we can add the following sub-categories:

Combination stains A combination of two or more of the above.
Dye stains Stains caused by dye products.
Special stains One-off stains that require special treatment (such as chewing gum).
Industrial stains Solidified concrete, mortar etc.
Chemical stains Stains caused by chemical spills (such as bleach).
Lacquer stains Lacquers that solidify (such as nail varnish).
Unknown stains Stains whose source cannot be identified.

Combination stains

Removal rating: Difficult
There are two types of combination stain. Type A stains have protein, grease/wax and dye elements; Type B stains have grease, wax and dye elements. Always treat the protein stain first, followed by the grease, then dye.

Type A

1 Rinse in cold water and soak in a cool biological (enzyme) detergent solution or pre-soak for 30 minutes.
2 Apply washing-up liquid or biological (enzyme) detergent to both sides. Launder in the hottest water that is safe for the fabric.
3 Bleach if necessary.

Type B

1 Treat with a grease-solvent product, rinse and air dry.
2 Apply washing-up liquid or neat biological (enzyme) detergent to both sides of the stain and launder in the hottest water that is safe for the fabric.
3 Bleach if necessary.

Dye stains

Removal rating: Difficult
Dye pigment is found naturally in cherries and blueberries, and is added to other foodstuffs like mustard and blue ice lollies. Dye stains also occur if you have laundered non-colourfast clothes with lighter colours.

Nearly all dyes used in fabrics are synthetics, manufactured from petrochemicals or coal-tar distillates. After colour testing (see page 19), spot treat with methylated spirits or a specialist solvent product. Rinse and air dry, then launder in the hottest water that is safe for the fabric. If traces remain, bleach or use a specialist dye-removing product.

Special stains

This category is for stains such as scorch marks and those caused by chewing gum that do not fall into any specific grouping, or those that do, like protein grass stains, but require a unique treatment method. For treatment, refer to each stain individually in the A–Z section.

Tip
The plastic covers used by dry cleaners can turn fabric yellow over time – this applies especially to lighter-coloured fabrics. Remove the covers before storing clothing for any length of time.

Organic stains

These are stains resulting from natural, often atmospheric conditions, such as tarnish, mildew and alkaline stains.

Industrial stains

These are stains resulting from building or DIY work. Refer to the A–Z for treatments.

Chemical stains

These stains result from chemical spills. Refer to the A–Z for individual treatments.

Lacquer stains

Removal rating: Difficult
Lacquer is a solid that is manufactured to apply in a liquid form, which then dries rapidly. Unfortunately, if allowed to penetrate a fabric in its fluid state, lacquer will coat every single fibre with a plaster that can be impossible to remove, so do not allow it to dry out. Sponge off the excess and treat with acetone nail varnish remover on all fabrics except wool, rayon, silk, acetate, triacetate and modacrylic. These should be treated with glycerine and dry cleaned as soon as possible. If the lacquer has dried, scrape off as much as possible with your fingernail or the edge of a coin before treating as above.

Unknown stains

Try identifying first by smell. If you are still not sure, keep in mind the two big don'ts: heat sets protein stains; soap sets tannin stains. Always start with the mildest treatment, soaking in cold water. For more information on treatments, see Unknown Stains, page 119.

STAIN-REMOVAL TECHNIQUES

Before removing any kind of stain, there are two questions you should always ask:

1 What is the stain type?
Protein stains are the easiest to remove, but will set if you use hot water, iron or tumble dry. Tannin (wet) stains respond well to hot water, but will set if you use any kind of soap. Greasy (dry) stains respond well to a little neat washing-up liquid and a hot wash.

2 What is the fabric and does it need colour testing?
Read the fabric care label for colourfastness, and washing and bleaching instructions.

General rules

DO treat the stain promptly. On non-washable fabrics, take it to the dry cleaner as soon as possible, and always tell them about the stain.
DO work from the back of the stain, to avoid forcing it further into the fabric.
DO dry clean washable items if the stain is very large, or the fabric delicate or bulky.
DO test for colourfastness and fabric damage before applying solvent, vinegar, alcohol or any kind of bleach.
DO read the care labels on garments and upholstery, and the instructions on products.
DO begin with the simplest method if there are several ways listed to remove a stain.
DO store chemicals out of the reach of children and away from food products.
DO leave a removal product on the stain for the advised length of time, to do its work.
DO work from the outside of the stain inwards to prevent stains spreading.
DO launder after treating with stain removers.
DO realize that some stains cannot be removed.

DON'T use hot water, iron or tumble dry ink, sugar and protein stains – heat will set the stain. If unidentifiable, use cold water first.
DON'T use soap on tannin stains; they will set.
DON'T give up after one application. Little and often is the best route to success.
DON'T forget to rinse. Solvents are highly inflammable, so rinse thoroughly and air dry.
DON'T iron or tumble dry a stained garment.
DON'T bleach a stain in isolation – always soak the whole garment. Remember, bleach does all its work in 15 minutes, so soaking for any longer will simply weaken the fabric.
DON'T rub at liquid stain spots, as you will simply spread the stain further and might damage the fibres. Blot on stain remover with an absorbent white cloth.
DON'T use a coloured cloth on stains, as the colour might transfer into the stain. Use a clean white cloth or kitchen towels.
Danger DON'T use solvents on inflammable stains like petrol and diesel. NEVER put solvent-treated garments into the tumble dryer.
Danger DON'T mix products, especially bleach and ammonia – it could trigger a chemical reaction and poisonous fumes.

Commercial products

Stain sticks are handy because of their size, but applying neat biological (enzyme) liquid detergent before laundering will work just as well on easier stains. Red-wine solvent stain removers are useful as they work well on all sorts of red and tomato-based stains.

Applying stain remover
Don't use a large amount to do the job faster – apply less rather than more. Repeating the process will be far more effective.

How to spot treat

Treat a small area with an aerosol solvent spray, methylated spirits, a dry-cleaning solvent, a spot remover or specialist solvent.

Fabrics

1 Spray or saturate the front of the stain and leave to penetrate for the specified time.
2 Scrunch up kitchen towels or an absorbent white cloth and place it over the stain.
3 Soak a small area of white cloth with the solvent or alcohol.
4 Turn to the back of the fabric and gently feather, blot or dab at the stain with the soaked cloth. Work from the outside of the stain inwards, to avoid spreading it further.
5 The stain will transfer to the backing towels or cloth. As it does, move the backing towels or cloth to expose a clean area and continue.
6 Repeat until the stain disappears, then rinse thoroughly. When chemical solvents have been used, air dry before laundering.
7 Launder as appropriate for the fabric.

Carpets and upholstery

1 Clear up any excess with kitchen towels, a sponge or an absorbent white cloth.
2 If advised to colour test, do this on a hidden area of carpet. Better still, when new carpet is laid, keep a square of carpet in store.
3 Apply treatment as advised for each stain.
Soda water should be applied generously, dabbed on with an absorbent white cloth, and re-applied as necessary.
Shaving cream should be applied minimally. It causes a lot of foam that is difficult to rinse.
Bicarbonate of soda, cornflour or talcum powder should be applied generously and left to dry completely before vacuuming off.

Always follow the manufacturer's directions for chemical spot treatments. If advised to leave for a certain amount of time, it is crucial that you do this. Work from the outside of the stain inwards, to avoid spreading it further.

Tip
Use your electric toothbrush with an old head as a spot-cleaning tool.

Spot-treatment techniques

Feather Use short, light rubbing movements.
Blot or dab Press the solvent-soaked cloth over the stain and apply gentle pressure.
   For all spot-treatment techniques, move to a clean part of the soaked cloth as the stain comes off on to it.

Stain-removal chemicals

The common stain-removal chemicals are shown in the chart. For details, see page 15.

PRODUCT	MAY CONTAIN
Alcohol (rubbing)	Isopropyl alcohol (K)
Ammonia	Ammonium hydroxide
Carpet shampoo, carpet stain remover	Isopropyl alcohol (K)
Colour remover	Sodium hydrosulphite
Nail varnish remover	Acetone
Petroleum-based solvent and dry-cleaning fluid	Trichloroethylene (TCE), perchloroethylene (PERC) (K), petroleum distillates (S)
Rust remover	Oxalic acid, hydrofluoric acid
Turpentine	Terpene

Environmentalists claim that 150 chemicals found in domestic cleaning products could be connected to asthma, allergies and some serious illnesses. Some contaminants can remain in the air for up to a year.

Because manufacturers are not obliged to list all the contents of their products on the label, it is not always possible to know which products contain the known and suspected carcinogens. But it is increasingly possible to buy eco-friendly products that are guaranteed not to contain any of the dangerous chemicals.

Safety with chemicals

If you do have to use chemicals, proceed with caution, and if you are in any doubt at all, don't. Call in the professionals.

Danger Never inhale solvents, carpet stain removers, ammonia, bleach or other chemicals.
Danger Always wear rubber gloves. Wear a face mask with ammonia and carpet solvents.
Danger Make sure you are working in a well-ventilated area, away from children and animals, and that there are no naked flames nearby. Don't smoke.
Danger ACT FAST. If you get any chemical on your skin, rinse immediately with cold water. If you have any stinging reaction in your eyes or on your skin, visit your doctor or local hospital immediately.
Danger Never transfer chemicals from their original containers, as these carry all safety instructions and precautionary statements. Read the directions for use and the safety and first-aid instructions carefully.

Warning labels

Look out for the following precautionary labels on packaging:

Caution or **Warning** Used on most cleaning products and detergents. If the appropriate first aid is administered, the product is unlikely to cause permanent damage.

Danger Used on products such as drain cleaners and some heavy-duty solvent stain removers. These products contain dangerous chemicals, so take greater precautions.
Poison The strongest warning of all, rarely found on commercial products.

Chemical effects on fibres

Some chemicals will permanently damage some fibres, even if they are diluted.

Chlorine bleach Do not use on spandex, nylon or any protein-based fibres (silk, wool, leather, mohair).
Acetone Found in paint thinner and nail varnish remover, this should not be used on acetates, triacetates and modacrylics.
Dry-cleaning fluids Those containing perchloroethylene should not be used on polypropylene. There are other dry-cleaning fluids that can be substituted.

Laundering

Less, rather than more, detergent produces cleaner, softer clothes. Too much detergent will not rinse out properly; instead, the dirt granules from any stains will be redistributed evenly among the fibres. Manufacturers are generous in their recommendations, averaging out hard and soft water areas. Try using less and check the results.

A great many stains, especially grease and protein, can be removed by laundering, but it is important to use the right detergent.

Powders without built-in fabric conditioners work better on stains.
Liquid detergents dissolve faster in cool, hard waters and so are better for soaking heat-hating protein stains.

There is no other real difference between the liquid and powdered brands, but most liquid detergents have a lower phosphate content and so are better for the environment.

Don't give up if the stain is still there after washing. Use neat liquid detergent or make a paste from detergent powder and a little water, apply to both sides and re-launder.

Greasy stains won't respond to a long wash in cold water. Detergents do remove oil, but only for a certain amount of time. After that, the grease simply re-deposits itself.

Water temperature
Hot 50–60°C (120–140°F)
Warm 30–40°C (85–105°F)
Cold 20–25°C (65–75°F)

Water below 15°C (60°F) is too cold for detergents to be effective.

Dry cleaning
If you have to take a garment to the dry cleaner, point out the stain and say how it occurred. If they know what caused it, they will know how to deal with it – there are different dry cleaning fluids for different purposes.

Stain removal around the home

Carpets
Soda water is very effective in treating many everyday spills – the carbonated bubbles will lift the dirt to the surface. Do not pour directly from the bottle, as the pressure will force the stain further into the fibres. Instead, saturate the stain and keep blotting until it is lifted.

If you have a big, greasy spill, dab away the excess and sprinkle cornflour, bicarbonate of soda or non-perfumed talcum powder over the stain. Leave for several hours – overnight if possible – and then vacuum. If the stain remains, squirt a tiny amount of shaving cream over it and brush gently into the fibres.

Wipe away the excess foam with a clean, dry cloth and blot with a sponge dipped in cold water. Or apply a weak solution of washing-up liquid and water and blot into the stain.

Chemical stains are more of a problem. They may not appear until long after the spill, when a change in humidity, temperature, sunlight or moisture in the air occurs. Tiny, permanent bleach spots can be disguised by filling in the colour with a felt-tip pen.

Tip
When you have new carpet laid, always keep a few squares of the trim. These are useful for colour testing, but also for restoring the original colour – dampen the faded area and rub over with the surface of the square.

Upholstery
Look for the fabric care symbol, usually under the cushions on the main frame of a chair or sofa, to see if it is washable or dry clean only. The latter should be treated with dry-cleaning solvent; never use water or water-based products on dry-clean only fabrics. When you buy any new furniture, always ask for a swatch of the upholstery fabric so that you can test for colourfastness. If you do not have this, tip up the chair or sofa and test solvents on an underside hem – spray on and spot clean an imaginary stain using a dry cloth.

Loose covers are the only covers that should be removed for washing. Don't remove and wash the cover of a tightly upholstered cushion, even if there is a big zip at the back and the fabric is washable. Getting it back on is always awkward; if the fabric shrinks by only a few centimetres, it will be impossible. Even it doesn't shrink, you may ruin the line of the lay of the fabric, and even a slightly changed colour will ruin the look of the whole sofa.

If you stain a cushion, unzip the cover before treatment (but don't remove it) and put a few layers of scrunched-up kitchen towel or absorbent white cloth between the stain and the foam. Follow the spot-treatment method: blot, dab or feather at the stain – don't wipe.

Leather sofas will stain from liquids, body oils and perspiration, but if the stain is absorbed, it will often fade with time. Don't wash greasy spots with water. Generally, stains on leather should not be spot cleaned – instead, clean the whole surface. Rub non-perfumed soap on a soft wet cloth, lather up and wipe over the surface. Clean off with a damp cloth and dry with a separate soft cloth.

Duvets

Duvets with synthetic fillings can usually be laundered. But if you get a stain on a feather or down duvet, act fast. Shake it out until the stained area of fabric is not in contact with any feathers and treat the stain before it dries.

Always have feather duvets professionally cleaned. The dry-cleaning machines in launderettes may leave fumes trapped inside.

Pillows

Wash foam- and feather-filled pillows by hand in warm, soapy water. Rinse thoroughly by holding the pillow under the tap and squeezing until all soapy residue has gone.

Dry foam pillows in the airing cupboard. Feather pillows should always be air dried.

Mattresses

Tip mattresses on to their side before cleaning. Sponge blood stains with cold salty water; urine stains with cold water and washing-up liquid. Remove heavy stains with pepsin powder, available from pharmacies, or apply a paste of cornflour and water, leave until it has dried and brush off. Repeat as necessary.

Crystal and glass

Rub marks gently with half a lemon. Soak stubborn stains in white vinegar. Leave for 15 minutes, scrub and rinse.

To prevent glasses clouding up in the dishwasher, stack so that they can't rub up against each other. To remove marks, place a cup of white vinegar in the lowest part of the dishwasher and run for 10 minutes. Stop the cycle, add detergent and wash as usual.

This is a list of the most useful stain removers and where to find them:

REMOVER	WHERE
Soda water	supermarket
Bicarbonate of soda	supermarket/ pharmacy
White vinegar	supermarket
Lemon juice	supermarket
Borax	pharmacy
Glycerine	pharmacy
Washing soda	supermarket
Cream of tartar	supermarket
Epsom salts	pharmacy
Methylated spirits	hardware store
Salt	supermarket

Your basic chemical kit need only consist of:
Biological (enzyme) washing detergent This is useful as a pre-soak. Alternatively, you can use a biological (enzyme) pre-soak powder.
Red-wine solvent stain remover This is useful for all sorts of red stains.
Bleach Keep oxygen all-fabric bleach for general use; chlorine bleach for really tough stains on tough fabrics.

STAIN-REMOVAL PRODUCTS

Natural products

Here is a list of the natural, non-commercial stain removers we use in this guide, with information on what they are and the stains on which they can be used.

Alcohol

Rubbing alcohol is a very effective multi-purpose, tough stain remover. It also works well as a grease and tannin spot stain remover on non-washable fabrics. Dilute 1 cup alcohol in 2 cups water for use on acetates, triacetates and non-colourfast fabrics. Methylated spirits (known as meths) is widely available. Use colourless meths.

Alcohol works well on chalk, grass and ballpoint ink stains. For best results, soak overnight in a sealed plastic bowl with a tight lid to prevent the alcohol evaporating, then rinse and launder. White wine can work on fresh red wine stains: suspend the fabric, stain side down, over the sink and pour white wine all over the stain. Gin makes a good spot cleaner for silks and non-washable fabrics. **Danger** All rubbing alcohols are poisonous and highly inflammable. Wear protective gloves, colour test (see page 19) and rinse thoroughly. Denatured, rubbing and isopropyl alcohol are used in commercial stain removers. Unproven links have been made between isopropyl, found in some carpet and upholstery stain removers, and nasal and sinus cancers, so avoid inhaling.

Ammonia

Ammonia is sold as a liquid in bottles but is actually a gas, diluted in water for convenience. Although it is chemically reproduced for commercial purposes, it is a natural by-product of decaying animals, plants, bacteria and animal and human wastes. It is extremely poisonous and inhaling it can badly affect your lungs. Use it as a last resort, always wear gloves and a mask and make sure the room is well ventilated.

Ammonia is a useful alkaline antidote to acidic vinegar, lemon and bleach stains, and also works well on tough, greasy stains. Always colour test the fabric before use (see page 19), as ammonia can change the colour of some dyes. If this happens, soak the area, dab on some white vinegar and soak again. **Danger** Never mix with bleach or any other cleaning agents. Don't use on silks and wools.

Bicarbonate of soda

This is one of the miracle natural stain removers, with lots of uses around the home, from cleaning tiles to deodorizing fridges. Made from soda ash, it is a cheap and very effective non-toxic, abrasive stain remover.

Mixed with lemon juice, bicarbonate of soda makes a powerful all-purpose cleaner and stain remover for sinks, baths and kitchen surfaces. A paste of bicarbonate of soda and water left on a stain for 30 minutes will remove perspiration, stains on glass, cuff and mud stains, dirt from wallpaper and many others. Half a cup added to the laundry detergent tray helps to break down protein stains and is especially safe when laundering stained baby clothes and bibs. It is also very effective at removing stains and old odours from microwave ovens: dissolve 2 tablespoons in 1 cup water and cook on high for 3 minutes. Wipe off stains with a damp cloth.

Borax

A natural, mildly alkaline salt, formed by the evaporation of saline lakes, borax can be used as a household disinfectant, detergent, water softener and greasy stain remover.

Famous as a nappy pre-soak, borax neutralizes the ammonia smell of urine. Sprinkled on to a damp cloth, it can get rid of stains on tiles, sinks, drains, floors, windows, mirrors and painted surfaces. You can throw out your chemical cleaners and use borax diluted in water as a general cleaner for all of the above. To use as a carpet stain remover, mix a paste of 3 parts borax to 1 part cold water and rub into the stain, leave to dry to a powder and vacuum off. Use on jam, jelly and dried-on fruit stains, leave for 15 minutes and rinse off. For a general greasy stain pre-soak that is safe for woollens, dissolve 1 tablespoon borax in a bowl of warm water. **Danger** Borax is an eye irritant – wear rubber gloves; keep your hands away from your face.

Bread

A slice of white bread removes dirty fingermarks from walls and fresh dirt marks from non-washable fabrics. It is also useful as an instant sponge at the dinner table. Immediately soak a slice of bread in soda water and place it over the stain. If done quickly enough, this will even work well on nasty-looking stains like beetroot.

Cigarette ash

The fine ash from burnt cigarettes makes an excellent ultra-light abrasive for removing alcohol stains from wooden furniture. Non-smokers may prefer to buy rottenstone from a hardware store. Mix with a little lemon juice or linseed oil to make a paste. Take a clean cloth and gently rub in the direction of the grain, wipe with linseed oil and repeat.

Citric acid

A safe, organic, white crystalline powder, this is the same acid that is found in lemons, grapefruits, oranges and other fruit. However, nearly all citric acid is manufactured from the fungus *Aspergillus niger*, by the fungal fermentation of sugar solution. You can buy it in packets from hardware stores. It oxidizes rust and is a very good, non-toxic way to remove stains from toilet bowls. Sprinkle all over and leave for an hour, scrub and flush.

Citrus oil

A safe, organic, pale yellow liquid, citrus oil is a manufactured biodegradable solvent that occurs naturally in citrus peel oil. Steam-distilled citrus oil can be used as a non-toxic replacement for toxic chlorinated solvents, found especially in tar and asphalt stain removers and graffiti stain removers. Buy it from the hardware store to use as a pre-wash treatment for stubborn grease stains.

Cornflour

The dried residue of corn grains, cornflour is a natural thickening agent used in cooking, but is also a highly versatile greasy stain remover. It works on both washable and non-washable fabrics including wool and silk, as well as on upholstery and carpets. Rub it into the stain, leave for 30 minutes and brush off.

Cream of tartar

A natural by-product of the wine-making process, this white crystalline powder comes from the sediment left at the bottom of the barrels after fermentation. It makes a good, natural pre-wash soak for whites like tablecloths and napkins. Dilute 2 tablespoons cream of tartar in 1 litre (2 pints) warm water and soak for 30 minutes. Mix to a paste with lemon juice to make a spot stain remover – leave for 30 minutes and rinse.

Denture cleaning tablets

These contain an oxygen bleaching agent called sodium perborate monohydrate, which is an excellent tannin stain remover for white cottons. Buy it from the dental section of the pharmacy, dissolve as directed on the packet and either apply as a spot stain remover with a soft cloth or soak for 1 hour.

Epsom salts

This pure mineral (magnesium sulphate soda crystals) has been used around the home for hundreds of years. It works well on tile stains. Mix equal parts Epsom salts and washing-up liquid, apply and scrub with a brush.

Eucalyptus oil

A natural antiseptic, eucalyptus oil comes from eucalyptus leaves. It helps to remove greasy, oily stains. Apply with a clean white cloth to tar stains after softening with glycerine.

Glycerine

A colourless, thick liquid, glycerine is an emollient, helping to maintain moisture levels. It dissolves in alcohol and water but not in oil, which is why it is such a good natural solvent – the stains will dissolve into glycerine more effectively than they will into alcohol or water. Make your own tannin stain remover by mixing 1 part glycerine and 1 part washing-up liquid in 4 parts water. Vegetable glycerine is available in most health-food stores.

Hairspray

The alcohol in hairspray works well on ink stains. Colour test before applying (see page 19) and use a non-aerosol type. Spray over, then agitate the fabric under running water.

Lemon juice

This is a natural, mild bleach with excellent stain-removing properties. After colour testing (see page 19), apply directly to the stain and leave to dry, if possible in sunlight. This will work on both washable and non-washable fabrics (but always colour test first), old red wine and fruit stains and on stains on marble surfaces. Mix to a paste with bicarbonate of soda for general cleaning and stain removal on kitchen surfaces, sinks, tiles and baths. For heavy staining, mix in a little flour and leave overnight. Mix with borax to make a paste to treat stained toilet bowls. Leave on overnight and then scrub. Mixed with salt, lemon juice is a powerful rust remover. Wet the rust, sprinkle with salt and then with lemon juice. Leave for 1 hour and then scrub off.

Linseed oil

Also known as flax oil, linseed is a natural vegetable oil obtained by pressing flax seeds. To remove water marks from wooden tables and furniture, mix linseed oil with an equal volume of turpentine and rub in with a soft cloth. Mixed with lemon juice, it makes an excellent general-purpose furniture cleaner.

Meat tenderizer

An enzyme-based powder that breaks down proteins, use on fresh blood stains: rub on, leave for 15 minutes and rinse in cold water.

Milk

The active enzymes in milk, responsible for breaking down the proteins that turn it sour and, eventually, into cheese, also work remarkably well on some stains. It makes a very effective soak for ballpoint ink, red juice and newsprint stains. Saturate the fabric and leave for 2–4 hours, then rinse thoroughly.

Onion

Onion's acidic chemicals work well on stains on leather. Slice in half and rub over leather shoes, furniture or clothing, then polish up.

Potato

Potatoes are natural enzyme stain sticks. Slice in half and rub over the (dry) stain before laundering. This also works as a quick spot dirt remover on non-washable fabrics. To remove rust from cooking tins, dip half a potato in salt or bicarbonate of soda and rub.

Pumice stone

A feather-light volcanic rock, pumice stone is highly porous, like a sponge. It is an excellent stain remover for ceramic and porcelain sinks and toilets. Dampen and rub hard over the stain, keeping the stone moist to avoid scratching. Do not use on metal or aluminium.

Rottenstone

A very fine abrasive powder, rottenstone is used to polish lacquered or varnished surfaces after coarse rubbing with pumice stone. Available from hardware and paint shops, rottenstone works well on alcohol stains on wooden surfaces. Mix with a little lemon essential oil or linseed oil to make a paste. Take a clean soft cloth and gently rub in the direction of the grain. Wipe with some neat lemon or linseed oil and repeat. Cigarette ash can be used as a substitute for rottenstone.

Salt

Salt not only absorbs oils but kills bacteria. A cold salt-water soak will break down protein stains and is the first thing to do with a blood stain. If sprinkled over wet tannin stains, salt absorbs excess liquid and prevents the stain penetrating further. It can be made into a paste with a little warm water to use on non-washables and upholstery. It works especially well on wine stains, which should be sprinkled liberally with salt immediately. Mixed to a paste with lemon juice, salt will also remove mildew stains.

Shaving cream

A good stand-by spot remover. Dampen the stain with water first, then squirt over shaving cream and rub with a soft cloth or old toothbrush. Rinse thoroughly. It makes an excellent emergency upholstery and carpet spot shampoo. Use sparingly: a tiny squirt will produce a lot of foam which must be rinsed off.

Soap

A sodium salt of an organic acid, soap is a surfactant – by reducing the surface tension, it increases the spreading and wetting properties of a liquid. It has been our main cleaning agent since the ancient Romans discovered that heating organic animal fat with inorganic wood ash resulted in the water combining with the grease for easy removal. It should never be used on tannin stains or they will set.

Soda water

This is a safe, clean way to get rid of liquid stains on clothes and carpets. After soaking the stain, the tiny bubbles in the soda water literally lift the dirt with them as they rise. Be sure to saturate the stain – the more water that gets down into the fibres, the more bubbles there will be to lift out the dirt. Work from the back of the stain, when possible.

It works well on perfume stains, ointments, suntan lotion, red wine (apply salt afterwards), coffee, yogurt, milk and cream.

Talcum powder

A grease-absorbing mineral useful for oil and grease stains if you have no cornflour or bicarbonate of soda to hand. Rub gently into the stain, leave for 30 minutes and brush off.

Tea tree oil

A natural antiseptic and disinfectant from the leaves of an Australian plant, *Melaleuca alternifolia*. It is often used as an ingredient in organic, eco-friendly cleaning products. To clean mould off garden cushions and fabrics, mix 2 teaspoons tea tree oil into 2 cups water, dab on and leave – do not rinse off. The stain and tea tree smell will disappear in 2–3 days.

Toothpaste

White, non-gel toothpastes are absorbents that contain the latest in stain-removing technology. They make good spot removers for blood, red wine and most of the non-oil based stains. Whitening toothpastes are good for white fabrics only, as some contain active whitening ingredients. However, these toothpastes also work well on dark spot stains on metal surfaces.

Turpentine

This solvent is made from pine oil and is sometimes described as 'distilled trees'. Used as a thinner for oil paints, varnishes and enamels, turpentine (turps) is good on difficult oil-based stains like asphalt and tar. It is also useful for removing dirt, wax and grease stains from walls and paintwork.

Danger Turpentine contains terpene, which is inflammable and toxic, so use turps only in a well-ventilated area.

Washing soda

A hydrated sodium carbonate, washing soda is a natural product from the same family as bicarbonate of soda. It makes an excellent substitute for chemical-solvent stain removers, as it does not give off toxic fumes but neutralizes odours instead. It is very good for greasy stains such as wax, lipstick and petroleum oil. Use as a soak, or as a spot stain remover by mixing to a paste with water.

Danger Washing soda is caustic, so always wear rubber gloves. Don't use it on fibreglass, waxed floors or aluminium as it will strip away the surface layer.

Washing-up liquid

Washing-up liquid is an excellent grease and stubborn protein stain remover. Apply directly to both sides, then rinse in hot water for greasy stains, cool for protein stains, agitating the back of the fabric together. Use colourless, unperfumed, phosphate-free brands.

White vinegar

White vinegar is a natural, mild bleach that dissolves dirt and grease and acts as a water softener. As it is 5 per cent acetic acid, vinegar makes an excellent bleach substitute without the noxious chemicals or fumes. Vinegar can be used neat to spot treat colourfast fabrics, or diluted – ½ cup to 4.5 litres (1 gallon) water – as a general soaker. It works particularly well on many tannin stains, grass, mildew, rust and suntan oil. Apply warm vinegar to baths, sinks and showerheads, leave for 30 minutes and any stains will scrub off easily. A boiling solution of 1 part vinegar to 6 parts water will remove stubborn mud marks from white socks: boil for 5 minutes, then leave overnight before rinsing. Mixed with equal parts olive oil, vinegar will remove water stains from wooden furniture.

Tip
When using white vinegar, add a few drops of essential oil to make it smell nice – lemon and lavender oils both work well.

Chemical

Here is a list of chemical stain removers used in this guide.

Acetone

A very fast-drying liquid, acetone is one of the most powerful solvents available. Use it on nail varnish, typewriter correction fluid and some paint and glue stains. It evaporates quickly, so place the stained area over scrunched-up kitchen towels or an absorbent white cloth and apply to the back of the stain.

Danger Don't inhale, and keep it away from your eyes, nose and skin. Don't use it on acetate, triacetate or modacrylic fabrics.

Amyl acetate (banana oil)

This is not oil from a banana but a liquid mixture of amyl acetate and nitrocellulose, which smells of banana. Used as a solvent and flavouring agent, it is good for removing glue from non-acetate fabrics. Scrunch up an absorbent cloth and place the front of the stain over it while you dab on the wrong side.

Danger Use amyl acetate in a well-ventilated area and don't inhale.

Bleach

Before using bleach, check the garment label to make sure the fabric is safe for bleach and colour test (see page 19).

3 per cent hydrogen peroxide The mildest bleach and generally safe for all fabrics. It is not the hair bleach hydrogen peroxide, which should never be used as a stain remover.

All-fabric bleach (sodium perborate, also known as oxygen bleach) Milder than chlorine bleach (see below), this is generally safe for all fabrics and colours. Oxygen bleach is the most environmentally friendly of all the chemical bleaches.

Chlorine bleach (5.25 per cent sodium hypochlorite) This is the strongest bleach and should always be diluted before use. Don't use it on wool, silk or spandex. Good for whites. Chlorine bleach can react with iron in hard water, turning the water brown and fabrics pink. It weakens with age, so do not keep it for longer than 6 months. Fresh bleach works fast: if the stain hasn't gone in 15 minutes, it never will.

Danger Always wear protective gloves.

Carpet spot shampoo

This is an aerosol foam for the direct treatment of carpet stains.

Danger Always wear a mask and gloves, as some carpet shampoos contain known or suspected carcinogenic chemicals.

Colour removers

These contain sodium hydrosulphite, which works as a reductive bleach to remove dyes from fabrics. Use it on whites, or if you intend to remove all colour. Read the instructions carefully and check that it is safe for the fabric.

Colour retainers

These contain an organic dye-fixing agent that helps to set colours on non-colourfast cottons and polyesters. It is recommended for laundering home-dyed fabrics.

Colour whitener

The sodium hydrosulphite and anhydrous sodium carbonate in this product remove stains and whiten fabrics you can't bleach, such as net curtains and white nylon bras.

Detergent

Granular (washing powder)
Heavy-duty (liquid)

Granular and liquid detergents work in the same way, the only difference being that liquid detergents dissolve much faster and in lower water temperatures than powder ones. They are therefore better for cold-water soaks and cool washes. Biological detergents are enzyme based and do remove more stains, but even better results will be obtained if you learn to identify and remove stains before laundering. Built-in fabric conditioners and bleaches may hinder stain removal, so it is best to add these separately as needed.

Do try to use a low-phosphate brand of detergent. If you use non-phosphate eco-friendly products, you can usually make up for the extra expense by using less, especially in soft water areas – too much detergent actually makes your clothes dirtier. If you are in a hard water area, add ½ cup borax to the dry soap tray or to the liquid detergent. 'Ultra' means highly concentrated, so you can use even less of these detergents.

Dry-cleaning solvent or spot remover

Dry-cleaning solvent is a liquid that contains no water but lots of chemicals. Environmentally damaging perchloroethylene (PERC) and trichloroethane (TCA) have been removed from most products but remain in some, so check the label. Other toxins such as petroleum solvent, petroleum hydrocarbon, petroleum distillate and naphtha may be present.

Danger Follow the manufacturers' instructions carefully. Never put a garment in the dryer until all traces of solvent have been removed.

Dye remover

Use if you get colour run by laundering non-colourfast clothes with lighter colours. But first, try laundering again immediately, before they dry out, in the hottest water for that fabric, using a bleach that is safe for the fabric.

Nail varnish remover

The main ingredient in nail varnish remover is propanone, also known as acetone. Because pure acetone dries so quickly, some nail varnish removers contain oil. For stain removal, you should always use the non-oily variety to avoid producing a grease stain. As well as removing lacquer stains, nail varnish remover also gets fruit dye stains off fingers.

Danger Don't use nail varnish remover on acetate, acrylic or triacetate.

Paint and varnish remover

This is a highly inflammable cocktail of toxic solvents, used for removing acrylic and oil-based paints. It may include the suspected carcinogens isopropyl alcohol, trichloroethane and methylene chloride.

Danger Older products may also include benzene, a known human carcinogen, and should not be used.

.

Pre-treatment products

What these products contain and claim depends on the basic stain type. Leave all liquid removers on the stain for several minutes, but do not let them dry out.

Danger Never mix two products together, as they can create noxious fumes.

Aerosols These are petroleum-based solvents for general use. They are excellent on old greasy stains like gravy, oil and butter.

Pump sprays These are detergent based; good for almost all stains except grease-based.

Pre-soak products and stain sticks These are detergent or digestant (enzyme) based, depending on their stain speciality: acid is for tannin stains; alkaline for protein stains.

Dry-cleaning solvents These are extremely toxic and can be flammable. Remove thoroughly from the fabric before air drying.

Rust removers

These will remove mud and dirt as well as rust. Available from hardware stores, some are for white fabrics only, so be sure to check the label first.

Danger Rust removers are highly poisonous liquid solvents containing hydrofluoric acid and oxalic acid, so handle with care and follow all safety instructions exactly.

Tile cleaners

Some tile cleaners contain lye, which is sodium hydroxide (caustic soda) or potassium hydroxide (caustic potash). It is also present in some drain and oven cleaners. Alternative organic tile cleaners are available, or you can use bicarbonate of soda, washing soda or borax.

Danger Protect your skin and eyes and do not inhale.

Trisodium phosphate (TSP)

Manufactured for washing down exterior surfaces before painting, you can buy TSP in hardware stores. Use it diluted in warm water to remove very stubborn blood stains.

Danger Follow all safety instructions carefully, as TSP can burn the skin and cause severe eye damage.

White spirit (hydrocarbon solvent)

A clear solvent mixture of mineral salts used for paint thinning and removing grease, white spirit works well as a spot treatment for glue stains, correction fluid marks and stubborn crayon marks.

Danger White spirit is toxic and highly flammable. Do not inhale, and if you get any on your skin, wash it off immediately with soap and water.

CLEANING GUIDE FOR FABRIC TYPES

After identifying the stain type, always read the care labels on the fabric to be treated. If in any doubt at all, do a quick colour test on a hidden seam or inside pocket.

Reading the labels

Bleaching

 Safe for chlorine bleach.

 Not safe for chlorine bleach.

Dry cleaning

 Dry clean only.

 Safe for dry-cleaning solvent.

 Safe for all types of dry-cleaning fluid.

For all the above, you can use the dry-cleaning washer in the launderette.

 Specialist dry cleaning needed; do not put in launderette machines.

 Specialist dry cleaning needed with solvent 113. You may have to shop around to find a specialist dry cleaner who can deal with this kind of fabric.

Ignoring the labels

Sometimes it is possible to launder garments that are labelled dry clean only.

Manufacturers can be over-cautious in their recommendations. Proceed with caution and use common sense. If in any doubt, DON'T.

If you have a bad stain on a coloured fabric that nothing will shift, it might be possible to use a stronger bleach without damage. Always colour test first on a hidden seam or inside pocket.

Dry cleaning

Dry-clean only labels are usually found on garments made from the fabrics listed below. You will also find dry-clean only labels on garments made from a combination of fabrics that have different laundering requirements – lined suits, for example. Always have feather duvets professionally cleaned.

After dry cleaning, leave the fabric out to air for a few hours before putting it away.

felt	silk and viscose
fur	chiffon
gabardine	some linens
hessian	tweed
most suedes	upholstery satin
old chintz	velvets and wools
serge	velvet brocade

Fabric conditioners

Conditioners soften fabrics, reduce static and creasing and make ironing easier, but detergents with built-in conditioners are not as effective on stains as those without. Use a separate conditioner so that you have a choice when you have a stained washload.

Colour testing

Dark blues and reds are the colours that are most likely to run. If you are in any doubt, do this quick test. With a cool iron, press a damp cotton handkerchief over a damp hem or inside seam. Then check to see if any colour has transferred to the handkerchief.

A–Z of fabric care

Drying and ironing instructions have only been given when fabrics require specific care.

Acetate and triacetate

Made from cellulose wood extract treated with acetic acid, acetates and triacetates usually have a silky look. Acetates usually need to be dry cleaned, though some can be hand washed at a warm 40°C (105°F) or cold in the machine. Triacetates can generally be machine washed. Don't use biological (enzyme) detergent on either and never wring out, twist, rub or spin dry. Don't use pre-treatment solvents or white vinegar – they will dissolve acetate. Don't soak coloured acetates other than those that are solution dyed.

Triacetate is more thermoplastic than acetate, which means it can be ironed and creases can be pressed into it – acetate will melt at the touch of a hot iron.

Acrylic

This is a washable, synthetic, wool-like fabric. Wash at a warm 40°C (105°F). Some acrylic/wool mixtures are hand wash only. Rinse in cold water to minimize creases. Don't drip dry or the fabric will stretch, and don't iron while still damp as it will become misshapen. Don't bleach.

Angora

Wool made from the hair of the angora goat (wool made from the angora rabbit has to be labelled as such), it is sometimes blended with nylon for easier care. Hand wash in lukewarm water with a woollens liquid soap or hair shampoo. Don't wring, rub or twist the fabric while washing. Dry by pressing out the water in the sink and rolling in a towel, before re-shaping and leaving to dry on a flat surface.

Steam over the surface with an iron, not allowing it to touch the fabric. Fluff up by brushing with a teasel brush.

Braid

Braid is not washable. Remove stains on silver braid with bicarbonate of soda – sprinkle on and leave overnight, then brush off. Remove stains on gold braid with a mixture of cream of tartar and stale breadcrumbs.

Brocade

A richly woven, satin-like silk made on a jacquard loom. Traditional brocade is often patterned with metal thread and should be dry cleaned only. Modern brocade is frequently made from artificial fibres and some of these can be washed. Hand wash very gently to prevent the pile design flattening. Don't wring. Iron over a towel on the wrong side of the fabric.

Broderie anglaise

An embroidered white cotton with decorative oversewn holes. It is usually safe to wash broderie anglaise following the instructions on the garment to which it is attached. Don't wash with garments with zips or hooks and eyes, which could get caught in the delicate holes and cause permanent damage.

Buckram

This is a heavily starched cotton. Curtains that contain buckram must be dry cleaned, as it will lose its stiffness if washed.

Calico

A lightweight, tightly woven cotton, often with tiny flowers. Wash as for cotton.

Candlewick

This is a cotton or wool/synthetic mix. Wash as for nylon.

Canvas

Originally all-cotton or linen, but now nearly always a cotton/synthetic mix, canvas is a tough, very tightly woven fabric. Scrub at stains with detergent and warm water. Colour test: if the results are fine, machine wash in cold water and tumble dry on warm; if not, dry clean.

Challis

This is a very soft cotton, rayon or wool with a brushed surface. Hand wash as for wool.

Cheesecloth

A very light cotton. As colours are likely to run, hand wash only and don't wring. Iron while damp.

Chiffon

A very delicate sheer silk, synthetic or silk/synthetic mix. Silk/viscose mixes should be dry cleaned. Hand wash other types in warm water. Iron while damp.

Chintz

This cotton has a glazed finish with big, bold designs. Dry clean old chintz; new chintz can be washed, but don't rub. Rinse in cold water and iron while damp.

Corduroy

A tough cotton/cotton mix. Despite its toughness, you should treat corduroy delicately to avoid damage to the pile. Blot stains with a wet cloth, and never rub or you could do permanent damage. If the pile is crushed, treat as for velvet.

Hand or machine wash corduroy, depending on the type. Wash inside out to protect the pile from rubbing against other fabrics. Iron while damp, on the wrong side.

Cotton

A versatile natural vegetable fibre, cotton is often mixed with other fibres and treated with fireproof or waterproof finishes. It is tough, naturally absorbent and easy to clean.

Most cottons have been pre-shrunk: those with looser weaves are more likely to shrink. Check that denim has been pre-shrunk before machine washing for first time and always wash jeans inside out to avoid streaking.

Nearly all white cottons can be machine washed at high temperatures and will take chlorine bleach, but always check the label. Wash coloureds and whites separately; wash coloureds on a cool wash in case they run. Hand wash delicate cottons like organdie and batiste in warm water with detergent. Don't use soap on flame-resistant finishes.

Tip
Always wash baby clothes separately. A cup of lavender-scented white vinegar added to the final rinse will get rid of any traces of uric acid and leave the clothes feeling beautifully soft.

Damask

A jacquard-weave fabric that comes in linen, silk, cotton, wool or a blend of these.

Silk, wool and the thicker fabrics should be dry cleaned. The thinner fabrics can be hand washed in cool water with detergent.

Down

Down is the very soft under-feathers of ducks and geese. It should be dry cleaned. Because fumes could become trapped and then breathed in while you sleep, never dry clean in the launderette – always go to the professionals. If you wash duvets and pillows in the washing machine, read the care label instructions carefully: the water temperature will depend on the fabric covering the down.

Down dries very slowly, so tumble dry on a low temperature rather than air dry. Fluff up at intervals throughout the drying process and make sure it is completely dry.

Felt
A thick, dense fabric, felt is not woven but pressed by heat. It is usually made from wool. Dry clean only.

Flannelette
This fabric can be cotton or synthetic, with a plain or twill weave. Generally, you should treat flannelette a little more gently than for other cottons/synthetics, as you would for wool. Check the label – some flannelettes must be dry cleaned.

Dry on a cool dryer setting, but **DON'T** allow it to dry completely in the dryer or wrinkles will set in.

Fur
Real fur must be dry cleaned. Some fake furs can be laundered – check the label.

Gabardine
This tightly woven twill can be made from worsted wool, cotton or synthetics.

Follow the care label instructions for cleaning. Synthetics are generally machine washable and can go in the tumble dryer; wool and cotton may be dry clean only.

Hessian
A heavy, plain fabric usually woven from jute. Dry clean only.

Jersey
A stretchy knitted fabric originating from the island of Jersey. Because of the way it is knitted, in a circular or warp method, jersey has a remarkable crease-resistant quality and washes and wears very well.

Some jerseys must be dry cleaned. Synthetic jersey is machine washable.

Lace
Lace can be made from natural cotton, linen or synthetic fibres. Spot treat stains before washing. Hand wash with detergent in a water temperature suitable for the fabric type. Never rub lace. Rinse well and don't wring, then reshape and pin down to dry. If lace has to be ironed, iron over a towel. Don't use bleach on lace and never tumble dry.

Lawn
Lawn is a soft, limp, fine-combed cotton or cotton/synthetic mix fabric. Hand wash only. Iron while damp.

Leather
Leather is tough, hardwearing and versatile. Leather with a dull finish is particularly susceptible to stains and is best treated with a specialist protector before wearing. Light stains can be removed with a mild, warm solution of washing-up liquid. After colour testing (see page 19), apply to the stain and leave for a few minutes before wiping off.

Spot clean ballpoint ink with milk or white spirit, or use a leather cuticle remover – spot it on to the stain, leave for 10 minutes, then spot clean with a soft, clean cloth. Don't use dry-cleaning spot remover on leather.

Linen
A strong natural fibre that comes from the inside stem of the flax plant. It is very hard-wearing and can withstand high temperatures.

Pre-shrunk linens can be put in the washing machine on a short warm wash cycle, but always colour test (see page 19) and look for the word 'pre-shrunk' on the label. To be safe, linen clothing should be dry cleaned. Stains can be removed from colourfast linens by soaking in an oxygen bleach for 15 minutes. Don't use chlorine bleach.

Iron while still damp. Air drying is a better option for linen – tumble drying can set creases, making it impossible to iron.

Mohair

A wool made from the hair of the angora goat (see Angora), this fibre too is sometimes blended with nylon for easier care. Generally, you can hand wash mohair as for wool, but check the label first.

Net

This fabric is made from nylon. Shake net vigorously before washing, as dirt gets caught in the little holes. Hand wash with soap in warm water. For heavy stains, soak in a pre-treatment net-whitening product.

Nylon

Light, strong and dirt resistant, nylon often needs no ironing. This makes it an extremely practical and popular fabric. Most nylon is machine washable at 50° or 60°C (120° or 140°F). White nylon will go grey if the water is too hot – this is particularly so with white bras, which should always be washed at a cool temperature. If this does happen, try soaking in a pre-treatment net-whitening product to restore whiteness; don't bleach nylon. Always turn nylon garments inside out before laundering to reduce pilling (eruptions of small, fur-like balls of fibre).

Because nylon is so good at repelling water, it needs a longer soaking time than cottons and linens. Leave nylon to soak for an hour or so before laundering in hot water with detergent on a particularly dirty load.

Nylon repels water-based stains, but absorbs grease stains and perspiration. Small grease spots on nylon can often be removed by putting a little neat washing-up liquid on both sides of the stain and rubbing gently with your fingers before laundering as usual.

Polyester

Polyester is a synthetic that is often blended with natural fibres for easy care. Be sure to check the label, but most polyesters can be machine washed at 60°C (140°F) for whites, and at 50°C (120°F) for colours. Washing polyester fabrics in very hot water will cause damage to the fibres.

Rayon

The most common type is viscose rayon. It is a highly absorbent fabric, not as strong as wool, cotton, silk or linen. Liable to shrink when it dries and stretch when it's wet, viscose rayon often requires dry cleaning. Treated rayons, called high wet modulus (HWM) rayons, can be laundered. Washable rayons are sensitive to chemicals and alkaline detergents, and should be treated with care.

Satin

Originally made from silk, most satin is now made from synthetic fibres. Hand wash, launder or dry clean – check the label. Dry clean upholstery satin. Iron washable satin while damp, on the wrong side.

Serge

Old serge is made from wool; modern serge is a cotton/synthetic mix. Dry clean only.

Silk

Silk is a natural, soft fibre that stains more readily than probably any other fibre.

Most silks must be dry cleaned, though some chemically treated, washable silks must never be dry cleaned – check the label. Some of the tougher, synthetic silks can be laundered in the machine or hand washed in warm, soapy water, as directed on the label. Never use biological (enzyme) detergents, and never rub wet silk. If it is badly stained, take it to the dry cleaner immediately. Use citrus oil as a greasy spot stain remover on silk. Iron while damp, on the wrong side.

Perspiration stains are very difficult to remove from silk. Don't allow them to dry – rinse out while still fresh and acidic.

Sugar stains can be tricky on silk. On wedding dresses, for example, always point out any spills to the dry cleaner, as they can dry to become invisible. After a period of storage, they will caramelize into brown spots that cannot be removed by dry cleaning.

Suede

This is a soft, brushed leather. Generally, suede is dry clean only, though a few types can be hand washed in warm soapy water – check the label. Surface marks can be removed from suede by rubbing with another piece of suede. Spot clean stains on suede with white vinegar.

Towelling

This is cotton with a high absorbency factor. It can usually be machine washed. Wash new dark-coloured towels separately for the first few times to avoid colour run. For white detergent stains on dark-coloured towels, machine wash in water softener or bicarbonate of soda. **DON'T** use fabric conditioner as it will reduce the absorbency of the fabric.

Tweed

This fabric can be made from wool or synthetic materials. Wool tweed should be dry cleaned only. Some synthetic tweeds can be hand washed – check the label.

Velour

A soft, velvet-like mixture of natural and synthetic fibres. Many velours can be machine washed at 40°–50°C (105°–120°F), but check the label.

Velvet

Velvet comes in many densities, from thick curtain weights to fine lingerie textures. Many velvets are machine washable – check the label. Always launder velvet inside out to protect the pile from rubbing against other fabrics. Silk velvet and heavy furnishing velvet are dry clean only. If you take a stained curtain to be dry cleaned, don't forget to take its matching pair – even a slight colour change will be very noticeable.

Following spot treatment, if the pile has flattened in the stain area, stretch out the fabric and hold it at both ends well away from the stain area, then place this over a steaming kettle spout.

Viscose

See Rayon.

Viyella

A manufactured blend of 80 per cent cotton and 20 per cent wool, viyella was one of the first blended fabrics ever created. Hand wash in warm water or machine wash on a cool minimum wash.

Wool

Wool comes in many textures and synthetic fibre blends. Pure wool is highly absorbent, soft and warm; it doesn't lose its shape and is very good at repelling stains. Cashmere is a very expensive, fine, soft wool that comes from the undercoat of cashmere goats.

Some wools and wool blends can be machine washed at 40°C (105°F) – check the label. Because wool is a stretchy fibre, it's best not to wear woollens immediately after laundering; leave for a day or so to allow the garment to return to shape.

ACID Chemical

Spills from acids such as citric acid and battery acid will stain quickly and permanently if not treated immediately.

Removal
Difficult

 Sprinkle bicarbonate of soda over the stain. Dip a clean cloth in cold water and moisten the area. Leave until it is no longer bubbling and rinse thoroughly in warm water.

Alternatively, hold the stained area over an open bottle of ammonia – the fumes will neutralize the acid. Rinse thoroughly.

 There is no chemical treatment to remove acid stains.

ADHESIVE Greasy

These stains are the creamy, rubbery glue residues left by sticky labels on clothes or rubber cement on surfaces.

Removal
Moderate

 Harden the glue on the fabric by covering the stain with a bag of ice cubes or putting in the freezer for 1 hour. Scrape off as much excess adhesive as possible with a spoon or blunt knife.

Sponge the area with eucalyptus or cooking oil to soften the fibres. Leave for 15 minutes, then apply washing-up liquid. Rinse and repeat as necessary.

On surfaces, squirt a little washing-up liquid on to the rubber cement and wipe off with kitchen towels or an absorbent white cloth.

 Freeze and scrape as above, then spot treat with grease-solvent stain remover or specialist adhesive solvent, blotting at the back of the stain (see page 7). Rinse the solvent thoroughly from the fabric and air dry, then launder with biological (enzyme) detergent.

Amyl acetate can be used on non-acetate fabrics and upholstery; for acetate fabrics and upholstery use white spirit.

Sponge non-washable fabrics with dry-cleaning solvent, repeating as necessary. If the stain persists, take to the dry cleaner as soon as possible.

ALCOHOL **Tannin**

Apart from the obvious red wine and beer stains, alcohol stains are often invisible, but are identifiable by smell.

Removal

Fairly easy, if treated quickly. Alcohol reacts with some fabric dyes. If the area has changed colour, this will probably be impossible to restore. Alcohol stains that have oxidized with heat and/or with age are impossible to remove.

 Spot treat with soda water, feathering at the back of the stain (see page 7).

If the stain persists, spot treat with a little washing-up liquid or liquid detergent, leaving for 5 minutes before feathering at the back of the stain. Rinse thoroughly before laundering.

Alternatively, dilute 2 tablespoons white vinegar in 1 cup water. Colour test and then spot treat, feathering at the back of the stain. Rinse thoroughly before laundering.

On non-washable fabrics, spot treat with soda water as above. If the stain persists, take to the dry cleaner and point out the stain.

On carpets and upholstery, spray or sponge with soda, water saturating the area. Keep blotting and reapplying soda water until the stain has lifted. If the stain persists, apply a weak solution of washing-up liquid and water and blot. Repeat as necessary.

Apply a small amount of biological (enzyme) liquid detergent to both sides of the stain, then soak in biological (enzyme) detergent solution for 30 minutes, before laundering in the hottest water that is safe for the fabric. If the stain persists, soak in all-fabric bleach for 15 minutes. If the stain still remains, and the fabric can take it, soak in chlorine bleach for 15 minutes.

On carpets and upholstery, dilute a small squirt of washing-up liquid in a cup containing 1 part 3 per cent hydrogen peroxide bleach to 6 parts cold water (NOT hair bleach, see page 16). Colour test, then sponge on to the stain and keep blotting until the stain has been removed. Rinse thoroughly.

ALGAE Organic

These are dark, mildew-like stains that appear on exterior surfaces such as roofs and boats, and damp interior places like bathroom surfaces and aquariums.

Removal
Easy with the right product, though some areas (such as swimming pool linings) are much more troublesome

 Dilute ½ cup white vinegar, ½ cup ammonia and a squirt of washing-up liquid in 4.5 litres (1 gallon) warm water. Scrub over the stain and rinse thoroughly.

 Mix 3 parts oxygen bleach to 1 part water and add a squirt of washing-up liquid. Scrub over the stained area and rinse thoroughly.

Wood deck cleaner containing oxygen bleach works well on roofs. Apply on a wet, dull day and leave to soak in as directed before brushing off.

For really stubborn stains, use a strong toilet-bowl cleaner containing hydrochloric acid.

 Follow the safety instructions exactly; rinse thoroughly.

ALKALI Organic

Two common types of alkali stain are murky dark brown stains on aluminium saucepans, and on the edges of concrete paths next to lawns, which are caused by weedkiller chemicals.

Removal
Easy, if treated immediately. If alkali stains have caused colour change, this is not reversible.

 Fill stained saucepans with 1 litre (2 pints) water and add ¼ cup white vinegar or lemon juice. Boil for 10 minutes, then pour away and scour with a soapy scouring pad. If the stain persists, add ¼ cup cream of tartar to 1 litre (2 pints) water and bring to the boil, simmer for 10 minutes and then scour.

On concrete paving, mix equal parts white vinegar and water in a bucket and drench the area. Scrub with a stiff broom.

 Soak saucepans in dilute hydrochloric acid overnight. Follow the safety instructions exactly; rinse thoroughly.

 Chemical treatments are available to treat alkali stains on concrete. If you have to use one of these, handle with care and follow the safety instructions exactly.

ALUMINIUM, STAINS ON Organic

Stains on aluminium saucepans appear as brown discoloration. Aluminium window frames exposed to salty air will develop black smears of oxide. Never use strong alkalis on aluminium. Acidic foods like tomatoes and green apples, washing soda and some dishwasher detergents will stain. Don't use scratchy metal utensils. When using a soap scourer, follow the grain of the metal. Don't use tough alkaline or acid cleaners on anodized aluminium, and wait for it to cool before cleaning.

Removal
Easy

 Dilute 1 tablespoon borax in 500 ml (1 pint) water, pour into the stained saucepan and leave to soak for 1 hour.

Alternatively, fill with 3 parts white vinegar to 1 part water, or 2 teaspoons cream of tartar to 1 litre (2 pints) water, and boil for 15 minutes.

To remove hard-water tidemarks on saucepans, fill with water, add a sliced lemon and boil for 20 minutes.

 On exterior and non-cookware aluminium, such as window frames stained by salt air, buy a tin of metal restorer from a car accessory store. It will get rid of rust, oxidization, acid salt stains and tarnishes.

ANTI-PERSPIRANT Chemical

Anti-perspirant produces a pale, powdery or lightened shade of the fabric on the underarm area of clothing.

Removal
Can be difficult to remove, especially from silk if it is not taken to the dry cleaner as soon as possible. If you sweat a lot and are wearing silk for a special occasion, think about using sweat shields to protect the fabric.

 Mix ½ cup bicarbonate of soda, ½ cup salt and a few drops of cold water to make a paste. Cover the stain and leave for 30 minutes. Rinse off with cold water.

If the anti-perspirant has changed the fabric colour, dab fresh stains with ammonia and rinse thoroughly. For woollens, dilute ammonia with equal parts cold water. For old stains, dab with white vinegar, then launder in the hottest water that is safe for the fabric.

On non-washable fabrics, apply bicarbonate of soda paste as above and leave for 30 minutes, then sponge off. If the stain persists, take to the dry cleaner.

 Make a paste from biological (enzyme) pre-soak powder and lukewarm water. Spot treat, leaving for 5 minutes, then dab the back of the stain (see page 7). Rinse with cold water, soak in biological (enzyme) detergent solution for 30 minutes, then launder in the hottest water that is safe for the fabric.

ASPHALT Dye

This black-grey sticky, tarry substance can be trodden into carpets or get on to clothing. If asphalt itself is stained with oil from your car, you will have to cut out the area with a masonry chisel and patch over.

Removal
Moderate

 If asphalt gets on to clothing, first harden it off in the freezer for 30 minutes or so. Scrape and pick off as much as possible with your fingernails and a blunt knife, taking care not to damage the fabric fibres. Cover both sides of the stain with liquid detergent and work it into the stain. Leave for 15 minutes and rinse.

 After freezing and scraping as above, soak the clothing for 15 minutes in all-fabric or chlorine bleach solution, as is safe for the fabric. Rinse and launder.

Alternatively, spot treat with a dye-solvent stain remover, dabbing at the back of the stain (see page 7). Rinse the solvent thoroughly from the fabric and air dry before laundering. If the stain persists, rub in biological (enzyme) liquid detergent. Leave this on and launder with biological (enzyme) detergent in the hottest water that is safe for the fabric.

On carpets, blot up as much asphalt as possible with kitchen towels. Colour test, then apply 3 per cent hydrogen peroxide bleach (NOT hair bleach, see page 16) and dab alternately with wet and dry cloths.

AUTOMOTIVE OIL Greasy

Automotive (car) oil is refined petroleum, a thick brown liquid that stains in greasy brown blobs.

Removal
Moderate – it requires some perseverance. Oil stains left longer than 24 hours on polyester, nylon or nylon/polyester blends will be very difficult to remove.

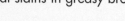 Dab up as much excess oil as possible with kitchen towels or an absorbent white cloth, then sprinkle the stain with bicarbonate of soda, cornflour or talcum powder and rub in gently. Leave for 30 minutes, then wipe off with a dry flannel facecloth. This method works on both washable and non-washable fabrics.

Alternatively, work a little washing-up liquid into both sides of the stain. Leave for 5 minutes before soaking in a bucket of water to which ½ cup washing-up liquid has been added. Leave for 30 minutes.

If the stain persists, mix bicarbonate of soda with a little cold water to make a thick paste, apply to the stain and leave for 30 minutes or until it has dried in completely, then brush off.

Launder in the hottest water that is safe for the fabric in a 50/50 detergent/bicarbonate of soda wash.

For overalls and clothes covered in oil, drench in cola before putting into the washing machine.

On carpets and upholstery, dab and sprinkle with powder as before. Leave for several hours – overnight if possible – and then vacuum. If the stain persists, squirt a tiny amount of shaving cream over it and brush gently into the fibres with an old toothbrush. Wipe away excess foam with a clean dry cloth and blot with a sponge dipped in cold water.

 Dab and sprinkle with powder as before to absorb excess oil, then rub biological (enzyme) detergent into both sides of the stain on dry fabric. Leave on and launder with biological (enzyme) detergent in the hottest water that is safe for the fabric.

If the stain persists, soak in all-fabric bleach solution for 15 minutes, rinse and launder. If the stain still remains, and the fabric can take it, soak in chlorine bleach solution for 15 minutes, rinse and launder.

DANGER Don't use solvents – this oil is highly inflammable.

DANGER Don't tumble dry, even after rinsing – always air dry.

AVOCADO **Protein**

Avocado leaves green, greasy-looking stains.

Removal
Easy

DON'T use hot water, tumble dry or iron until the stain has been removed completely – heat sets avocado stains.

 Scrape off as much excess avocado as possible with a spoon or blunt knife. Rinse under cold running water, gently agitating the back of the fabric against itself, then soak in cold water with liquid detergent for 1 hour. Don't launder the fabric until most of the stain is removed.

If the stain persists, soak for 30 minutes in a mix of 1 tablespoon borax to 500 ml (1 pint) lukewarm water, then launder. Don't soak woollens: instead, spot treat with the same borax solution (see page 7).

Launder with liquid detergent in warm water.

 Scrape and rinse as above. Soak in warm water with biological (enzyme) detergent or pre-soak. Don't launder until most of the stain is removed. Wash with biological (enzyme) liquid detergent in warm water.

BABY FOOD Protein or tannin

Meat and vegetable courses are protein stains, but fruit desserts and drinks are tannin stains. Launder baby clothes separately from other clothes.

Removal
Easy, if the stain is given the appropriate treatment before laundering. Vomit contains stomach acids, which can be difficult to remove if not treated immediately (see page 122).

DON'T use hot water, iron or tumble dry protein stains – heat sets them.

DON'T use soap on fruit and juice stains – soap sets them.

 Always have a bottle of soda water handy to treat immediate spills. Spot treat with soda water, feathering at the back of the stain (see page 7). Then soak in cold water, swishing the fabric around.

Unseasoned meat tenderizer is excellent for treating baby food stains – it has an enzyme in it that breaks down protein stains. Make up a paste with cool water, apply and leave for 1 hour. Rinse and launder.

For fruit and juice stains, stretch the fabric right side down over a sink, bowl or saucepan, securing with clothes pegs or an elastic band. Pour through the hottest water that is safe for the fabric from the back of the stain, from as high as possible without danger of splashing.

 Soak in warm water with biological (enzyme) detergent or pre-soak for 30 minutes. Soak really stubborn stains for 15 minutes in non-chlorine bleach. Rinse and launder with biological (enzyme) detergent.

BABY FORMULA Protein

Milk formula substitute for breast milk causes yellowy, milky stains. Note that if you have formula and breast milk stains, the latter contain fat and should be spot treated as for greasy stains.

Removal
Easy

DON'T use hot water, tumble dry or iron until the stain has been removed completely – heat sets baby formula stains.

 Soak fresh stains in cold water immediately, swishing the fabric around. Whites can be blotted with fresh lemon juice and left in the sun to dry.

Unseasoned meat tenderizer is excellent for treating baby formula stains – it has an enzyme in it that breaks down protein stains. Make up a paste with cool water, apply and leave for 1 hour. Rinse and launder.

For fatty breast milk stains, work a little neat washing-up liquid into both sides of the stain. Leave for 5 minutes before soaking in a bucket of water to which ½ cup washing-up liquid has been added. Leave for 30 minutes, then rinse and launder.

 Soak in warm water with biological (enzyme) detergent or pre-soak for 30 minutes. Soak really stubborn stains for 15 minutes in non-chlorine bleach. Rinse and launder with biological (enzyme) detergent.

Treat fatty breast milk stains with biological (enzyme) liquid detergent. Apply to both sides of the stain, then soak in warm water with biological (enzyme) pre-soak for 30 minutes. Rinse thoroughly and launder with biological (enzyme) detergent in the hottest water that is safe for the fabric.

BABY OIL Greasy

Baby oil is a non-toxic, clear mineral oil with a pleasant smell that leaves a faint, clear stain.

Removal
Moderate

 Dab up as much excess oil as possible with kitchen towels or an absorbent white cloth, then sprinkle the stain with bicarbonate of soda, cornflour or talcum powder and rub in gently. Leave for 30 minutes to allow the powder to absorb the oil, then wipe off with a dry flannel facecloth. This method works on both washable and non-washable fabrics.

Alternatively, work a little washing-up liquid into both sides of the stain. Leave for 5 minutes before soaking in a bucket of water to which ½ cup washing-up liquid has been added. Leave for 30 minutes.

If the stain persists, mix bicarbonate of soda with a little cold water to make a thick paste, apply to the stain and leave for 30 minutes or until it has dried completely, then brush off.

Launder in the hottest water that is safe for the fabric in a 50/50 detergent/bicarbonate of soda wash.

On carpets and upholstery, dab and sprinkle with powder as above to absorb excess oil. Leave for several hours – overnight if possible – then vacuum. If the stain persists, squirt a tiny amount of shaving cream over it and brush gently into the fibres with an old toothbrush. Wipe away excess foam with a clean dry cloth and blot with a sponge dipped in cold water.

 Dab and sprinkle with powder as above to absorb excess oil, then spot treat with grease-solvent stain remover, feathering at the back of the stain (see page 7). Rinse the solvent thoroughly from the fabric and then air dry before laundering.

Alternatively, rub biological (enzyme) liquid detergent into both sides of the stain. Leave this on and launder with biological (enzyme) detergent in the hottest water that is safe for the fabric.

BACON FAT Greasy

The grease from bacon dries into the fabric, leaving a yellow, fatty crust on the surface.

Removal

Moderate – may require some perseverance. Stains left for longer than 24 hours on polyester, nylon or nylon/polyester blends will be very difficult to remove.

DON'T iron until all traces of the stain have been removed.

 Dab up as much excess grease as possible with kitchen towels or an absorbent white cloth, then sprinkle the stain with bicarbonate of soda, cornflour or talcum powder and rub in gently. Leave for 30 minutes, then wipe off with a dry flannel facecloth. This method works on both washable and non-washable fabrics.

If the stain persists, mix bicarbonate of soda with a little cold water to make a thick paste, apply to the stain and leave until completely dry, then brush off.

Launder in the hottest water that is safe for the fabric in a 50/50 detergent/bicarbonate of soda wash.

On carpets and upholstery, dab and sprinkle with powder as above. Leave for several hours, then vacuum

 Dab and sprinkle with powder as above, then spot treat with grease-solvent stain remover, feathering at the back of the stain (see page 7). Rinse thoroughly from the fabric, then air dry before laundering.

BAKED BEANS Combination

Baked bean stains are tomato based, as with ketchup and tomato sauce.

Removal

Moderate

 Rinse as soon as possible under cold running water, holding the back of the stain under the tap and letting the water run through. Colour test, then dab white vinegar all over the back of the stain and rinse through again. Repeat several times.

Work liquid detergent into the back of the stain and launder in the hottest water that is safe for the fabric.

 Rinse as above. Spot treat with red-wine stain remover, dabbing at the back of the stain (see page 7). Rinse thoroughly from the fabric, then air dry and launder.

If traces of the stain remain, rub biological (enzyme) liquid detergent into both sides of the stain. Leave this on and launder with biological (enzyme) detergent in the hottest water that is safe for the fabric.

If the stain persists, soak in all-fabric bleach solution for 15 minutes, rinse and launder. If the stain still remains, and the fabric can take it, soak in chlorine bleach solution for 15 minutes, rinse and launder.

Dissolve 1 teaspoon biological (enzyme) detergent in 1 cup water. Saturate the stain and blot off with kitchen towels or an absorbent white cloth. Rinse, then launder in the hottest water that is safe for the fabric.

If the stain persists, soak for 15 minutes in all-fabric bleach solution. Rinse and then launder.

BEETROOT **Combination**

Beetroot leaves alarming-looking bright purple stains.

Removal
Moderate

 For whites, stretch the fabric right side down over a sink, bowl or saucepan, securing with clothes pegs or an elastic band. Cover the back of the stain with borax, then pour through the hottest water that is safe for the fabric, from as high as possible without danger of splashing.

For coloured fabrics, add 1 tablespoon borax to 500 ml (1 pint) warm water, soak for 1 hour and then launder. If you don't have any borax, soak in cold water immediately for 2 hours. Then, for all fabrics except woollens, rub washing-up liquid into the stain. Leave to soak for 30 minutes, then rinse and repeat as necessary. Rinse and launder.

If beetroot spills on a tablecloth, soak a slice of bread in soda water and lay it over the stain. If you don't have soda water to hand, use cool tap water.

On carpets and upholstery, spray or sponge with soda water, saturating the area. Keep blotting and reapplying soda water until the stain has lifted. If the stain persists, squirt a tiny amount of shaving cream over it and brush gently into the fibres with an old toothbrush. Wipe away excess foam with a clean dry cloth and blot with a sponge dipped in cold water.

 Soak in a solution of biological (enzyme) detergent and warm water for 1 hour. Rinse and launder with biological (enzyme) detergent.

On non-washable fabrics, sponge with cold water and take to the dry cleaner as soon as possible.

On carpets, dilute 1 cup 3 per cent hydrogen peroxide bleach in 1 litre (2 pints) water (NOT hair bleach, see page 16). Colour test, then spray the solution over the stain and keep dabbing with kitchen towels or an absorbent white cloth.

35

BERRIES Tannin

These stains can usually be identified by their colour and smell. Cranberry, strawberry and raspberry can all be treated as described below. Cherry and blueberry are dye stains – see individual entries.

Removal
Moderate

 Stretch the fabric right side down over a sink, bowl or saucepan, securing with clothes pegs or elastic band. Pour through the hottest water that is safe to use from the back, from as high as possible without splashing.

Fresh stains will usually disappear in a normal wash, the hottest that is safe for the fabric. If not, rub over a cut lemon, rinse and air dry in the sun.

Alternatively, mix equal parts white vinegar and the hottest water that is safe for the fabric, colour test and sponge over the stain. Rinse and air dry in the sun.

For old stains, rub in a little glycerine, leave for 1 hour and rinse. Apply one of the methods above.

 Wet the stain with cold water and apply a red-wine stain stick to both sides. Launder with biological (enzyme) detergent in the hottest water that is safe.

If the stain persists, soak in all-fabric bleach solution for 15 minutes, rinse and launder. If the stain still remains, and the fabric can take it, soak in chlorine bleach solution for 15 minutes, rinse and launder.

BIRD DROPPINGS Organic

These are white or purple streaky stains that literally appear out of nowhere!

Removal
Easy (white) to moderate (purple)

 Scrape off as much of the excess droppings as possible. Rinse under cold running water, gently agitating the back of the fabric against itself. Soak in cold water with liquid detergent for 1 hour. Don't launder until most of the stain has gone.

If the stain persists, soak for 30 minutes in a solution of 1 tablespoon borax to 500 ml (1 pint) warm water, then launder. Use to spot treat woollens (see page 7).

Launder with liquid detergent in warm water.

 Soak purple stains in cool water with biological (enzyme) pre-soak for 30 minutes. If the stain persists, dilute 1 cup 3 per cent hydrogen peroxide bleach in 1 litre (2 pints) cold water (NOT hair bleach, see page 16). Colour test, then spray the solution over the stain, dabbing with kitchen towels or absorbent white cloth.

For carpets and upholstery, use carpet stain remover.

BITUMEN Combination

Bitumen is a tar-like substance used in the building process for waterproofing and sealing. A methylated-spirit based stop-stain sealant will protect stone fireplaces from bitumen stains.

Removal
Difficult without chemicals, especially on concrete, which is porous and tends to soak up stains on contact

 Protect adjacent areas with polythene sheets. If fresh, leave until the bitumen has cooled. Cover with a bag of ice cubes, then chip off with a paint scraper or, for delicate surfaces like limestone, a wooden spatula. Scrub with scouring powder and rinse with clean water.

 Protect adjacent areas and scrape as above, then apply a specialist solvent product available from builder's merchants. Swab off the excess solvent immediately and leave as directed. If the stain is really stubborn, make a poultice with the solvent, seal the area with polythene sheets and leave for 4–8 hours.

BLEACH Chemical

Hydrogen peroxide hair bleach will dry out into anything from yellow to black. Chlorine bleach stains into white spots.

Removal
Difficult to impossible

 To neutralize the acid, rinse the back of the stain immediately under cold running water.

Colour test, then spot treat the stain with ammonia (see page 7). For woollens and silks, dilute the ammonia 50/50 with cold water. On non-washable fabrics, hold over the fumes from a bottle of ammonia.

Alternatively, make a paste with bicarbonate of soda and water and rub into the back of the stain. Rinse and repeat as necessary.

On carpets, rub bicarbonate of soda paste thoroughly into the stain, leave to dry and vacuum.

Yellowing of whites caused by using too much bleach, or a bleach reaction to hard water, is not removable. If yellowing has been caused by chlorine-bleached clothes that have been tumble dried without being rinsed properly, or an overheated dryer, laundering again immediately may be successful.

Tiny spots on carpets and cottons, linens and rayons can be disguised by filling in with felt-tip pen or ink.

 Generally speaking, there is no chemical that will remove bleach stains, but some specialist systems exist in the carpet-cleaning world. Consult a professional.

Yellowing of whites caused by too much exposure to sunlight can be corrected by chemical bleaching.

BLOOD Protein

Blood stains can be anything from bright red to dull brown, depending on freshness.

Removal

Fresh: Easy
Old: Moderate

DON'T use hot water or white vinegar – they will both set blood stains.

DON'T treat other people's blood stain without wearing protective rubber gloves. Examine these for tears and holes, and dispose of them afterwards.

 Soak in cold, strong salt water. Keep changing the soaking solution over a period of 30 minutes, until the water runs clear. Make a paste from salt and water and rub into what remains of the stain.

For small spots, spit on to a cotton bud or cottonwool ball and rub gently.

Clear gel hair shampoo also works well, especially on larger stains on sheets or mattresses. Pour all over the stain and scrub with a brush dipped in cold water, then rinse and launder. Make sure every trace of the stain has been removed before laundering, otherwise the hot water will set the stain. Take mattresses off the bed and put on their side for treatment. Hold woollens under cold running water to prevent the fibres clogging when you rub with shampoo.

For fresh, wet carpet stains, spray or sponge on soda water and rinse. Alternatively, make a paste from 3 parts borax to 1 part water. Sponge on to the stain, then leave to dry and vacuum off.

On non-washable fabrics, dilute 1 dessertspoon ammonia in 500 ml (1 pint) water and colour test, then dab on with a sponge and rinse.

For dried-in stains on carpets and upholstery, spray or sponge with soda water, saturating the area. Keep blotting and reapplying soda water until the stain has lifted. If the stain persists, apply a weak solution of washing-up liquid and water to the stain and blot. Repeat as necessary.

 Soak in cold salt water as above, then leave to soak in biological (enzyme) detergent for several hours, or overnight if the stain has set dry.

For blood stains on white carpets and upholstery, sponge up as much excess blood as possible, then colour test and dab with 3 per cent hydrogen peroxide bleach (NOT hair bleach, see page 16), followed by boiling water.

For really old, stubborn stains, and if the fabric can take it, soak in a warm solution of trisodium phosphate for several hours. Alternatively, apply hydrogen peroxide as above, let it bubble and repeat until the stain disappears.

BLUEBERRY Dye

The dye element present in blueberry makes it one of the toughest berry stains to remove. The other difficult one, requiring the same treatment, is cherry.

Removal
Difficult

 Mix a thick paste from borax and warm water, and spread it on the back of the stain. Leave for 30 minutes and then rinse.

Alternatively, colour test, then soak overnight in 1 cup milk with 1 teaspoon white vinegar. Rinse.

 Spot treat with red-wine stain remover, dabbing at the back of the stain (see page 7). Rinse thoroughly from the fabric and then air dry before laundering.

If traces remain, rub biological (enzyme) liquid detergent into both sides and launder with biological (enzyme) detergent in the hottest water that is safe.

If the stain persists, soak in all-fabric bleach solution for 15 minutes, rinse and launder. If the stain still remains, and the fabric can take it, soak in chlorine bleach solution for 15 minutes, rinse and launder.

BUTTER Greasy

Butter leaves a fast-penetrating, fatty yellowish stain. Melted butter is absorbed even more quickly.

Removal
Moderate

 Scrape off as much excess butter as possible with a blunt knife. Sprinkle with bicarbonate of soda, cornflour or talcum powder and rub gently into the stain. Leave for 30 minutes. Wipe off with a dry flannel facecloth. This works on washable and non-washable fabrics.

Alternatively, work a little washing-up liquid into both sides. Leave for 5 minutes, then soak in a bucket of water to which ½ cup washing-up liquid has been added. Leave for 30 minutes, then rinse and launder.

On carpets and upholstery, scrape and sprinkle with powder as above. Leave for several hours, then vacuum.

 Scrape and sprinkle with powder as above. Spot treat with grease-solvent stain remover, feathering at the back of the stain (see page 7). Rinse thoroughly from the fabric and air dry before laundering.

Alternatively, rub biological (enzyme) liquid detergent into both sides and launder with biological (enzyme) detergent in the hottest water that is safe for the fabric.

On carpets and upholstery, scrape and sprinkle with powder as above, then treat with dry carpet cleaner.

CABBAGE JUICE, RED Protein

Juiced cabbage, a common ingredient in health drinks, leaves pale purple stains.

Removal
Easy

DON'T use hot water, tumble dry or iron until the stain has been removed completely – heat sets red cabbage juice stains.

 Wipe off as much excess juice as possible, then rinse under cold running water, gently agitating the back of the fabric against itself. Soak in cold water with liquid detergent for 1 hour. Don't launder until most of the stain has been removed.

If the stain persists, soak for 30 minutes in a solution of 1 tablespoon borax to 500 ml (1 pint) lukewarm water and then launder as usual. Spot treat woollens and non-washables with the same borax solution as above (see page 7).

Launder with liquid detergent in warm water.

 Wipe off the excess and rinse as above, then soak in lukewarm water with biological (enzyme) detergent or pre-soak. Don't launder until most of the stain has been removed.

Launder with biological (enzyme) liquid detergent in warm water.

CALAMINE LOTION Combination

Used to soothe itchy skin, calamine lotion can leave pale yellow stains that dry to brown. These are likely to be found on sheets and bedding in addition to clothing.

Removal
Moderate

 Spot treat with a weak solution of washing-up liquid and warm water, blotting at the back of the stain (see page 7). Rinse in cool water, gently agitating the back of the fabric against itself, and then launder.

If the stains have dried into brownish marks, mix 1 part white vinegar to 2 parts water, colour test and then spot treat. Rinse in cool water and then launder as usual.

On carpets, carefully spot treat the stained area with methylated spirits, gently dabbing at the stain – don't rub the stain.

 Spot treat with grease-solvent stain remover, feathering at the back of the stain. Rinse the solvent thoroughly from the fabric and air dry before laundering.

Alternatively, rub biological (enzyme) liquid detergent into both sides of the stain. Leave this on and launder with biological (enzyme) detergent in the hottest water that is safe for the fabric.

On carpets, mix 2 tablespoons 3 per cent hydrogen peroxide bleach with 1 cup cool water (NOT hair bleach, see page 16). Colour test, then spray or lightly dab over the area, taking care not to rub the stain in any further. Rinse and repeat as necessary.

CANDLE WAX Greasy

Usually found in clusters of solid, cloudy circles, the hard bits of wax are easy to scrape off, but an oily stain may remain that is more difficult to remove.

Removal
Moderate

 Make sure the wax is hard. Cover with ice cubes or put in the freezer for a few minutes. Crack the surface and gently scrape with a blunt knife, then pick at the remaining bits with your fingernail. Place the fabric between kitchen towels and press the back of the stain with a warm iron. Keep moving the paper around as the wax is absorbed, until the paper remains clean.

Through this process, part of the stain may be forced into the fibres, leaving an oily-looking residue. If this happens, dab with methylated spirits. For nylon, dilute the methylated spirits 50/50 with water first, then rinse and launder.

On carpets and upholstery, chill with ice, then pick out as much wax as you can with a knife and your fingernails as above. Cover the wax with a towel or several layers of kitchen towel and apply a warm iron. Rub with methylated spirits before shampooing.

For tables, pick off the hard bits of wax, then wash down with a solution of 1 part white vinegar to 2 parts hot water.

 Harden and scrape off the excess as above, then apply an aerosol pre-treatment spray and scrub by hand with biological (enzyme) liquid detergent in very hot water.

If you use the ironing method above and are left with an oily spot, treat with spot stain remover before laundering in the hottest water that is safe for the fabric. If the stain persists, bleach with the strongest bleach solution that is safe for the fabric.

Treat non-washable fabrics with dry-cleaning solvent.

CAR DOOR GREASE Greasy

These oily black streaks appear on the sides of jackets and coats often without you noticing until you arrive at your destination.

Removal

Moderate – sometimes requires perseverance. Stains left longer than 24 hours on polyester, nylon or nylon/polyester blends will be very difficult to remove.

 Scrape off as much excess grease as possible with a spoon or blunt knife, then sprinkle with bicarbonate of soda, cornflour or talcum powder and rub gently into the stain. Leave for 30 minutes to allow the powder to absorb the grease, then wipe off with a dry flannel facecloth. This method works on both washable and non-washable fabrics.

Alternatively, work a little washing-up liquid into both sides of the stain. Leave for 5 minutes before soaking in a bucket of water to which ½ cup washing-up liquid has been added. Leave for 30 minutes.

If the stain persists, mix some bicarbonate of soda with a little cold water to make a thick paste, apply to the stain and leave for 30 minutes or until it has dried in completely, then brush off.

Launder in the hottest water that is safe for the fabric in a 50/50 detergent/bicarbonate of soda wash.

On carpets and upholstery, scrape off the excess as above. Dilute 1 tablespoon borax in 500 ml (1 pint) warm water. Sponge on to the stain, alternating with clean warm water as the stain is removed.

 Spot treat with a grease-solvent stain remover, dabbing at the back of the stain (see page 7). Rinse the solvent thoroughly from the fabric and air dry before laundering.

Alternatively, rub biological (enzyme) liquid detergent into both sides of the stain. Leave this on and launder with biological (enzyme) detergent in the hottest water that is safe for the fabric.

Sponge non-washable fabrics with dry-cleaning solvent. If the stain persists, take to the dry cleaner as soon as possible.

CARBON PAPER/RIBBON Combination

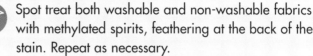

Carbon paper and typewriter ribbon leave black or red smudgy grease stains.

Removal
Difficult – requires time and effort. Work on the oily, wax part of the stain first, then the dye.

 Spot treat both washable and non-washable fabrics with methylated spirits, feathering at the back of the stain. Repeat as necessary.

If the stain persists, add 4 tablespoons ammonia to 1 litre (2 pints) warm water. Leave to soak for several hours. Rinse thoroughly. To neutralize all traces of the ammonia, mix a solution of equal parts white vinegar and water and spot treat or soak for 1 hour.

 Spot treat with methylated spirits as above, then rinse and soak for 30 minutes with biological (enzyme) detergent. Rinse thoroughly and launder with biological (enzyme) powder or liquid detergent.

If the the stain persists, soak for 15 minutes in all-fabric bleach solution and rinse thoroughly. If the stain still remains, and the fabric can take it, soak for 15 minutes in chlorine bleach solution.

CARPET GLUE Greasy

The synthetic clear, strong glue used in carpet laying creates clear, slightly yellowish stains.

Removal
Moderate

 Scrape off as much excess glue as possible with a blunt knife or old credit card, working from the outside of the stain inwards to avoid spreading it any further. Dabbing repeatedly with warm soapy water might be enough to remove small stains.

On non-delicate colourfast fabrics, dilute 1 part white vinegar in 10 parts boiling water and soak for 1 hour, then launder.

On concrete and brick surfaces, harden the glue by placing a bag of ice cubes over it and leaving for 30 minutes, then chip it off.

 Scrape off the excess as above, then spot treat with acetone liquid solvent (see page 7). Test first on an inconspicuous part of the fabric: don't use acetone on acetate, triacetate or modacrylic fabrics.

 DANGER Handle with care: acetone is one of the most powerful solvents. It is very fast drying and evaporates quickly – don't inhale.

CARROT JUICE **Protein**

These orange stains can be identified by smell.

Removal
Easy

DON'T use hot water, tumble dry or iron until the stain has been removed completely – heat sets carrot juice stains.

 Blot off as much excess juice as possible with kitchen towels or an absorbent white cloth, then rinse under cold running water, gently agitating the back of the fabric against itself. Soak in cold water with liquid detergent for 1 hour. Don't launder until most of the stain has been removed.

If the stain persists, soak for 30 minutes in a mix of 1 tablespoon borax to 500 ml (1 pint) lukewarm water, then launder. Spot treat woollens with the same borax solution (see page 7).

Launder with liquid detergent in warm water.

 Blot and rinse as above, then soak in lukewarm water with biological (enzyme) detergent or pre-soak. Don't launder until most of the stain has gone. Wash with biological (enzyme) liquid detergent in warm water.

CEMENT RESIDUE **Industrial**

These stains usually occur as small splatters left by builders.

Removal
Moderate

 Chisel off the cement using a hammer and bolster, keeping the bolster as horizontal as possible to avoid chiselling into the surface. Start with gentle taps and gradually build up just enough force to remove the cement. To clear the surface of marks after chiselling, scrub with a wire brush.

 You can buy specialist cement removers from the builder's merchant, but treat with caution: they contain an acid that breaks down cement, but it also attacks other surfaces like paving, limestone and marble. Always test on an inconspicuous area of the surface.

Wet the surface and apply as directed, which usually means leaving for 5–10 minutes. Don't use this product in the sun as it will dry too rapidly. Scrub off the cement with a wire brush and rinse thoroughly.

 DANGER It is vital to protect yourself if using this product: wear protective clothing, protective gloves and, crucially, eye goggles. Read the instructions thoroughly and follow them exactly.

CHEESE SAUCE Protein

These creamy yellowish marks consist of milk and cheese. Thick marks will dry to a crust.

Removal
Easy

DON'T use hot water, tumble dry or iron until the stain has been removed completely – heat sets cheese sauce stains.

 Scrape off any crusty residues with a blunt knife or old credit card. Rinse under cold running water, gently agitating the back of the fabric against itself, then soak in cold water with liquid detergent for 1 hour. Don't launder until most of the stain has been removed.

If the stain persists, soak for 30 minutes in a mix of 1 tablespoon borax to 500 ml (1 pint) lukewarm water and then launder as usual. Don't soak woollens: instead, spot treat the stain with the same borax solution (see page 7).

Launder with liquid detergent in warm water.

 Scrape and rinse as above. Soak in lukewarm water with biological (enzyme) detergent or a pre-wash stain soaking treatment. Don't launder until most of the stain has been removed, then wash in warm water using biological (enzyme) liquid detergent.

CHEWING GUM Special

This pink or cream sticky mess will be flattened to a disc-like appearance if left on a floor for any length of time.

Removal
Moderate

If you get chewing gum on a carpet, don't vacuum until every trace has been removed or it could damage your cleaner.

 Cover with a bag of ice cubes to harden the gum, or put in the freezer for an hour. The gum should then be brittle enough to crack off.

Spot treat whatever is left with white vinegar (colour test first) or methylated spirits, dabbing at the back of the stain (see page 7). Rinse thoroughly, and air dry if using meths, then launder.

Rub with egg white or liquid detergent and launder.

On carpet and upholstery, freeze and remove the brittle surface as above, then spot treat with white vinegar or methylated spirits.

 Freeze and remove the brittle surface as above, then spot treat with specialist chewing-gum solvent. Rinse the solvent thoroughly from the fabric and air dry before laundering.

 DANGER Lighter fuel also works as a spot-treatment solvent on gum, but is highly inflammable. Use with extreme caution and never on acetate or acetone.

CHOCOLATE Combination

Chocolate causes stains that are usually brown or white with a hardened crust. They are easy to confuse with excrement: if in doubt, identify by smell.

Removal
Moderate

DON'T use hot water, tumble dry or iron until the stain has been removed completely – heat sets chocolate stains.

 Scrape or blot off as much excess chocolate as possible with a spoon, blunt knife or kitchen towels, then spot treat with soda water, dabbing at the back of the stain (see page 7). Rinse under cold running water.

Alternatively, make the chocolate really brittle by holding a bag of ice over the stain or putting it in the freezer for 1 hour. Then hold the back of the stain under cold running water for at least 5 minutes.

Don't launder until most of the stain has been removed. Make a paste from powdered detergent and water and rub into both sides of the stain, then launder in warm water.

If the stain persists, colour test, then spot treat with ammonia, dabbing at the back. Rinse and launder.

 Scrape or blot off the excess as above, then spot treat with a specialist solvent or stain stick. Rinse the solvent thoroughly from the fabric and air dry, then launder with biological (enzyme) detergent.

If the stain persists, soak in all-fabric bleach for 15 minutes.

On non-washable fabrics, blot off the excess as above, then dry clean as soon as possible.

COCOA/HOT CHOCOLATE

Combination

These milky brown stains can be confused with excrement: if in doubt, identify by smell.

Removal
Moderate

DON'T use hot water, tumble dry or iron – heat sets cocoa stains.

 Immediately blot off as much excess liquid as possible with kitchen towels, then saturate the back of the stain with soda water and dab repeatedly with kitchen towels or an absorbent white cloth. Rinse the back of the stain under cold running water, gently agitating the back of the fabric against itself. Leave to soak in cold water with liquid detergent for 1 hour, gently agitating the back of the fabric against itself from time to time. Apply washing-up liquid to both sides of the stain and launder in the hottest water that is safe for the fabric.

If the stain persists, soak in a solution of 1 tablespoon borax to 500 ml (1 pint) water, then launder. Spot treat woollens with the solution (see page 7). Launder with liquid detergent in warm water.

On carpets and upholstery, spray or sponge with soda, water saturating the area. Keep blotting and reapplying soda water until the stain has lifted.

 Blot off the excess and treat with soda water as above. Soak in lukewarm water with biological (enzyme) detergent or pre-soak. Don't launder until most of the stain has been removed. Launder with biological (enzyme) liquid detergent in warm water.

COD LIVER OIL **Greasy**

Cod liver oil leaves a clear or yellowish greasy stain.

Removal
Difficult – if not treated immediately, it will be impossible to remove. A chemical solvent applied immediately gives the best chance of success. Stains left longer than 24 hours on polyester, nylon or nylon/polyester blends will be impossible to remove.

 Dab up as much excess oil as possible with kitchen towels or an absorbent white cloth, then sprinkle with bicarbonate of soda, cornflour or talcum powder and rub gently into the stain. Leave for 30 minutes to allow the powder to absorb the oil, then wipe off with a dry flannel facecloth. This method works on both washable and non-washable fabrics.

Alternatively, work a little washing-up liquid into both sides of the stain. Leave for 5 minutes before soaking in a bucket of water to which ½ cup washing-up liquid has been added. Leave for 30 minutes.

If the stain persists, mix bicarbonate of soda with a little cold water to make a thick paste, apply to the stain and leave for 30 minutes or until it has dried in completely, then brush off.

Launder in the hottest water that is safe for the fabric in a 50/50 detergent/bicarbonate of soda wash.

 Dab and sprinkle with powder as above to absorb excess oil, then spot treat with grease-solvent stain remover, feathering at the back of the stain (see page 7). Rinse the solvent thoroughly from the fabric and air dry before laundering.

Alternatively, rub biological (enzyme) liquid detergent into both sides of the stain. Leave this on and launder with biological (enzyme) detergent in the hottest water that is safe for the fabric.

On carpets and upholstery, dab and sprinkle with powder as above, then treat with dry carpet cleaner.

COFFEE Tannin

Coffee comes in a myriad of forms and all can be treated in exactly the same way – except coffee with cream, which is a combination stain.

Removal
Moderate

Coffee is a natural dye so should be treated as quickly as possible. Don't use any kind of soap – soap sets coffee stains.

 Rinse immediately in cold water. Stretch the fabric right side down over a sink, bowl or saucepan, securing with clothes pegs or an elastic band. Pour through the hottest water that is safe for the fabric from the back of the stain, from as high as possible without danger of splashing. If this doesn't work, sprinkle borax over the stain and repeat.

Alternatively, make a paste from powdered detergent and water and apply to the dry stain on both sides. Leave this on and launder in the hottest water that is safe for the fabric.

For stubborn, dried-in stains, spot treat with methylated spirits, dabbing at the back of the stain (see page 7). Rinse and launder. Or mix equal parts glycerine and warm water, leave to soak for 2–3 hours and rinse.

On carpets and upholstery, spray or sponge with soda water, saturating the area. Keep blotting and reapplying soda water until the stain has lifted.

 For stubborn stains, mix 1 part 3 per cent hydrogen peroxide bleach with 6 parts water and colour test (NOT hair bleach, see page 16). Soak for 30 minutes. Rinse and launder with biological (enzyme) detergent.

For creamy coffee stains, spot treat with grease-solvent stain remover or rub in biological (enzyme) liquid detergent. If using a solvent, rinse thoroughly from the fabric and air dry before laundering. If using detergent, leave this on and launder with biological (enzyme) detergent in the hottest water that is safe for the fabric.

COLLAR/CUFF SOIL Combination

These stains are much easier to remove if dealt with immediately. If you have an on-going problem, strips can be stuck on to the inside of collars to soak up all the oil and dirt.

 Shampoo naturally dissolves body oils. Rub hair shampoo all over the stain and launder.

Alternatively, make a thick paste from bicarbonate of soda and white vinegar, and colour test. Scrub with a toothbrush. Leave for 30 minutes, then rinse and launder in the hottest water that is safe for the fabric.

Removal
Moderate, depending on fabric – very difficult to remove from synthetic fibres if left for more than 24 hours.

DON'T use hot water, tumble dry or iron until the stain has been removed – heat sets the stains. Soaking in cold water won't help.

 Spot treat with stain stick or solvent spray (see page 7) – solvents work better. Leave on for 30 minutes, then rinse and air dry. Apply biological (enzyme) liquid detergent to both sides of the stain, then launder with biological (enzyme) detergent in the hottest water that is safe for the fabric. For whites, add ½ cup chlorine bleach to the first rinse.

COLOUR RUN IN WASH Dye

Colour run usually occurs when you launder a non-colourfast garment with lighter colours in a hot wash. Always wash whites separately and coloureds at a lower temperature. Don't leave wet clothes in the machine after washing. Soaking colourfast coloureds in white vinegar before laundering will keep them bright and intense.

Removal
Difficult

 Try washing immediately with washing soda in a permanent press cycle with hot water and a cool rinse.

Alternatively, stretch the fabric over a bowl, sink or saucepan and secure with clothes pegs or an elastic band, then leave under a dripping cold tap for 4–5 hours. Drain away as and when necessary, making sure the bowl is empty enough for the water to drip freely through the fabric.

Or colour test, then soak overnight in equal parts methylated spirits and ammonia, covering the bowl or bucket with clingfilm to make it airtight and prevent the gases escaping. Rinse thoroughly, air dry and launder.

 If the fabric can take it, launder again immediately with chlorine bleach.

Alternatively, soak coloureds and delicates in a biological (enzyme) pre-soak solution, before laundering with biological (enzyme) powder in the hottest water that is safe for the fabric.

Mix 3 parts 3 per cent hydrogen peroxide bleach with 1 part water (NOT hair dye bleach, see page 16) and colour test. Apply to the dyed area and place outside in the sun. Keep re-moistening until the stain has gone, then rinse and launder. This works well on silks, woollens and delicates.

Try using a dye remover. These products contain sodium hydrosulphite, which breaks down the dyes in the fabrics. Follow the instructions carefully – the chemicals can cause damage to buttons and zips.

Soak nets and white nylons in fabric whitener.

COOKING FATS AND OILS **Greasy**

These transparent to yellow greasy stains are found everywhere in the kitchen – on clothes, tea towels and oven gloves. They often dry into the fabric or surface to leave a yellow, fatty crust.

Removal
Moderate

Stains left longer than 24 hours on polyester, nylon or nylon/polyester blends will be very difficult to remove.

 Dab up as much excess oil as possible with kitchen towels or an absorbent white cloth. If cooking fat has hardened, scrape it off carefully with a blunt knife, working from the outside of the stain inwards to avoid spreading it any further. Sprinkle with bicarbonate of soda, cornflour or talcum powder and rub gently into the stain. Leave for 30 minutes, then wipe off with a dry flannel facecloth. This method works on both washable and non-washable fabrics.

Alternatively, work a little washing-up liquid into both sides of the stain. Leave for 5 minutes before soaking in a bucket water to which ½ cup washing-up liquid has been added. Leave for 30 minutes.

If the stain persists, mix bicarbonate of soda with a little cold water to make a thick paste, apply and leave until it has dried in completely, then brush off.

Launder in the hottest water that is safe for the fabric in a 50/50 detergent/bicarbonate of soda wash.

On carpets and upholstery, dab off or scrape and sprinkle with powder as above. Leave for several hours – overnight if possible – then vacuum. If the stain remains, squirt a tiny amount of shaving cream over the stain and brush gently into the fibres with an old toothbrush. Wipe away excess foam with a clean dry cloth and blot with a sponge dipped in cold water.

 Dab up or scape and sprinkle with powder as above. Spot treat with grease-solvent remover (see page 7). Rinse thoroughly from the fabric and air dry. Launder.

Alternatively, rub biological (enzyme) liquid detergent into both sides and launder with biological (enzyme) detergent in the hottest water that is safe for the fabric.

COPIER TONER **Combination**

Copier toner comes in liquid or powder form and causes dense black stains.

 If it's a powder spill, shake out as much as possible. Don't touch the stain, as the grease on your fingers will spread it. Sponge the back with warm soapy water.

Spot treat washable and non-washable fabrics with methylated spirits, feathering at the back (see page 7).

Removal
Difficult

If the stain persists, add 4 tablespoons ammonia to 1 litre (2 pints) warm water and soak overnight. Rinse thoroughly. To neutralize the ammonia, soak for 1 hour in a solution of equal parts white vinegar and water.

 Spot treat with methylated spirits or a pre-treatment solvent spray, rinse and soak for 30 minutes with biological (enzyme) detergent, then rinse thoroughly again. Launder with biological (enzyme) powder or liquid detergent in warm water.

If the stain persists, soak for 15 minutes in all-fabric bleach solution and rinse thoroughly. If the stain still remains, and the fabric can take it, soak for 15 minutes in chlorine bleach solution.

COPPER, STAINS ON Tarnish

Tarnish stains on copper saucepans and cookware are common. To keep copper shiny, polish frequently and wipe down with a salt/white vinegar solution after each use.

Removal
Easy to moderate, depending on how long the stain has been there

 Light, recent stains can be removed by rubbing with half a lemon dipped in salt.

Alternatively, pour white vinegar over the surface, sprinkle with salt and rub in. Rinse with warm water and polish dry.

A third method is to mix a paste from bicarbonate of soda or cream of tartar and lemon juice and wipe all over the stain. Leave for 5 minutes and rinse.

Small items without decorative trims can be boiled in a mixture of equal parts white vinegar, salt and water. Simmer for 30 minutes, then rinse, dry and polish up.

For bright copper, make a polish by mixing equal parts white vinegar and lemon juice. For dull copper, mix equal parts rottenstone and olive oil.

To treat 'bronze disease' patches of corrosion, mix hot white vinegar or lemon juice with salt and rub over the stain. Rinse immediately in soapy water.

 Apply a specialist copper cleaning powder and follow the instructions. This will not work where the tarnish has penetrated a crack in the lacquer: the lacquer will first have to be removed with acetone, the treatment applied, then the lacquer reapplied. Remove lacquer by immersing in a bowl of boiling water to which ½ cup washing soda has been added. Peel off the lacquer. Alternatively, rub with acetone or alcohol.

CORRECTION FLUID Lacquer

Most of these petroleum-based products are difficult to remove, leaving a thick white stain. You can buy water-based correction fluids that can be removed in a normal detergent wash.

Removal
Difficult – impossible on some fabrics. As it dries, it will coat each individual fibre, covering it with an irremovable plaster.

 Scrape off as much as possible with your fingernail or the edge of a coin. Rub washing-up liquid into both sides of the stain, then launder in the hottest water that is safe for the fabric.

If you get correction fluid on your hands, remove with pumice stone.

 Sponge the back of the stain with amyl acetate (banana oil) or white spirit. Rinse and air dry, then repeat as necessary.

Alternatively, apply biological (enzyme) liquid detergent to both sides of the stain and launder with biological (enzyme) detergent in the hottest water that is safe for the fabric. Take non-washable fabrics or stubborn stains to the dry cleaner as soon as possible and tell them to treat as a solvent-based paint stain.

COUGH SYRUP Tannin

These sticky syrup stains are usually yellowy, orangey or red and strong-smelling.

Removal
Easy

 Spot treat the back of the stain with soda water or soak the fabric immediately in cold water. Gently agitate the back of the fabric against itself or hold the back of the stain under cold running water and let it run through for 5 minutes or until the stain disappears.

On carpets and upholstery, spray or sponge with soda water, saturating the area. Keep blotting and reapplying soda water until the stain has lifted.

 Soak in all-fabric bleach in cool water for 15 minutes.

For old, stubborn stains, spot treat with red-wine stain remover, dabbing at the back of the stain (see page 7). Rinse the solvent thoroughly from the fabric and air dry before laundering.

Alternatively, rub biological (enzyme) liquid detergent into the stain on dry fabric. Leave this on and launder with biological (enzyme) detergent in the hottest water that is safe for the fabric.

CRAYONS AND COLOURED PENCILS Combination

These oily or waxy stains can include dye of any colour.

Removal
Moderate

 Colour test, then apply white vinegar to the front of the stain and gently scrub the back with an old toothbrush. This method also works on walls, tables and carpets, in these cases scrubbing the front of the stain.

Alternatively, cover both sides of the stain with liquid detergent on dry fabric. Leave for 1 hour, then launder in the hottest water that is safe for the fabric.

Another method is to dab white spirit over the stain and soak for 1 hour in a solution of 2 parts water to 1 part glycerine. Rinse and launder in the hottest water that is safe for the fabric.

On surfaces, cover the stain area with non-gel toothpaste, then leave for 15 minutes and wipe off. Repeat as necessary.

 Spot treat with grease-solvent stain remover, feathering at the back of the stain (see page 7). Rinse the solvent thoroughly from the fabric and air dry before laundering.

Alternatively, rub biological (enzyme) liquid detergent into both sides of the stain. Leave this on and launder with biological (enzyme) detergent in the hottest water that is safe for the fabric.

If the stain persists, soak in all-fabric bleach solution for 15 minutes, rinse and launder. If the stain still remains, and the fabric can take it, soak in chlorine bleach solution for 15 minutes, rinse and launder.

On tables, walls and floors, spray solvent on a clean cloth and wipe.

On non-washable fabrics, don't attempt to spot treat as you may make it worse – take straight away to the dry cleaner.

CREAM Protein

These thick, white milky stains should be treated immediately. If allowed to dry, cream (and milk) stains give off a horrible smell.

Removal
Easy

DON'T use hot water, tumble dry or iron until the stain has been removed completely – heat sets cream (and milk) stains.

 Spray the back of the stain with soda water or soak the fabric immediately in cold water. Gently agitate the back of the fabric against itself, or hold the back of the stain under cold running water and let it run through for 5 minutes or until the stain disappears.

On carpets and upholstery, spray or sponge the stain with soda water, saturating the stained area. Keep blotting and reapplying soda water until the stain has lifted.

 Spot treat with stain stick (see page 7), then launder with biological (enzyme) detergent in warm water.

If the stain persists, rub biological (enzyme) liquid detergent into both sides of the stain on dry fabric and then launder.

On non-washable fabrics, dab with lukewarm water and treat with dry-cleaning spot remover.

For old, stubborn stains, rub biological (enzyme) detergent into the stain and leave to soak in cool water for 4 hours, gently agitating the back of the fabric against itself from time to time.

CURRY Combination

Curry can stain in any shade of yellow, red or brown and is best identified by smell.

Removal
Moderate

 Scrape off as much of the excess curry as possible with a spoon or blunt knife, then saturate in warm water and wring out as much excess water as possible. Rub glycerine all over the stain and leave for 1–2 hours. Rinse, and repeat as necessary.

On carpets and upholstery, scrape off the excess as above. Dilute 1 tablespoon borax in 500 ml (1 pint) warm water. Sponge on to the stain, alternating with clean warm water as the stain is removed.

 Scrape off the excess as above, then rub biological (enzyme) liquid detergent into both sides of the stain and launder with biological (enzyme) detergent in the hottest water that is safe for the fabric.

If the stain persists, soak in all-fabric bleach solution for 15 minutes, rinse and launder. If the stain still remains, and the fabric can take it, soak in chlorine bleach solution for 15 minutes, rinse and launder.

Take non-washable fabrics to the dry cleaner as soon as possible.

DEODORANT Special

Deodorant stains do not contain the same chemicals as anti-perspirant (see page 27), so are slightly easier to remove. The stains look similar: powdery, or discoloration of the fabric in the underarm area.

Removal
Moderate

DON'T iron deodorant stains – heat sets them.

 Colour test and then dab white vinegar over both sides of the stain before laundering.

Alternatively, make a paste from equal parts bicarbonate of soda and salt mixed with a few drops of cold water. Spread over the stain and leave for 15 minutes, then rinse and launder.

Alternatively, cover both sides of light stains with liquid detergent on dry fabric and launder in the usual way.

If the fabric has changed colour, sponge with ammonia. If treating silks and woollens, dilute the ammonia with equal parts water.

On non-washable fabrics, blot with bicarbonate of soda/salt paste as above, then blot off. If the stain persists, take to the dry cleaner as soon as possible.

 Apply stain stick. Leave this on and then launder.

Make a paste from biological (enzyme) pre-soak powder and lukewarm water, cover both sides of the stain and leave for 5 minutes. Then soak in biological (enzyme) detergent for 30 minutes before laundering in the hottest water that is safe for the fabric.

For stubborn stains, make a paste from all-fabric bleach and cold water and rub on to both sides of the stain. Wrap the garment in clingfilm or put it in a plastic bag and leave for 6–7 hours or overnight. Rinse and launder with biological (enzyme) detergent in the hottest water that is safe for the fabric.

DIESEL FUEL Greasy

Diesel fuel leaves dark brown greasy stains.

Removal
Moderate

Diesel stains left longer than 24 hours on polyester, nylon or nylon/polyester blends will be very difficult to remove.

 Dab up as much excess diesel as possible with kitchen towels or an absorbent white cloth, then sprinkle with bicarbonate of soda, cornflour or talcum powder and rub gently into the stain. Leave for 30 minutes, then wipe off with a dry flannel facecloth. This method works on both washable and non-washable fabrics.

Alternatively, work a little washing-up liquid into both sides of the stain. Leave for 5 minutes, then soak in a bucket of water to which ½ cup washing-up liquid has been added. Leave for 30 minutes.

If the stain persists, mix bicarbonate of soda with a little cold water to make a thick paste. Apply and leave until it has dried in completely, then brush off.

Launder in the hottest water that is safe for the fabric in a 50/50 detergent/bicarbonate of soda wash.

On carpets and upholstery, dab and sprinkle with powder as above. Leave for several hours – overnight if possible – then vacuum. Dilute 1 tablespoon borax in 500 ml (1 pint) warm water and sponge on to the stain, alternating with clean warm water as the stain is removed. If it persists, squirt on a tiny amount of shaving cream and brush gently into the fibres with an old toothbrush. Wipe away excess foam with a clean dry cloth and blot with a sponge dipped in cold water.

 Dab and sprinkle with powder as above, then rub biological (enzyme) detergent into both sides on dry fabric and launder with biological (enzyme) detergent in the hottest water that is safe for the fabric.

If the stain persists, soak in all-fabric bleach solution for 15 minutes, rinse and launder. If the stain still remains, and the fabric can take it, soak in chlorine bleach solution for 15 minutes, rinse and launder.

DANGER Extreme caution must be taken when dealing with diesel and petrol stains, as they make clothing more inflammable than normal.

DANGER Don't use solvent-based stain removers.

DANGER Don't put in the tumble dryer, even after rinsing – always air dry.

DYES, RESTORING **Dye**

Some stains will remove dyes from fabrics, and some stain-removal techniques (if not colour tested first) will remove dyes from fabrics.

Removal
Moderate

 Ammonia restores colour on over-bleached fabrics and to anti-perspirant and deodorant stains. It doesn't work on all fabrics and dyes, so colour test first. Mix equal parts ammonia and water and apply to the stain, rinse well and launder. Don't use on woollens and silks. If the ammonia has reacted badly with the fabric, soak immediately, dab on white vinegar and soak again.

To restore colour to carpets lightened by stains like urine, dilute 1 teaspoon ammonia in 1 cup water, sponge on and rinse.

 If the faded patch is beyond repair, remove the colour from the fabric with a colour remover and re-dye. Check that the product is safe for the fabric and follow the instructions exactly.

 DANGER Don't mix ammonia with bleach or any other cleaning agents.

! DANGER Colour removers should be used with extreme care. Wear protective gloves.

EGG **Protein**

Raw or cooked, egg stains are bright and messy, but they are easily removed.

Removal
Easy

DON'T use hot water, tumble dry or iron until the stain has been removed completely – heat sets egg stains.

 Spot treat the back of the stain with soda water or soak the fabric immediately in cold water. Gently agitate the back of the fabric against itself or hold under cold running water and let it run through for 5 minutes.

On carpets and upholstery, spray or sponge with soda water, saturating the area. Blot and reapply.

 Apply stain stick. Leave this on and launder with biological (enzyme) detergent in warm water.

Alternatively, rub biological (enzyme) liquid detergent into both sides of dry fabric, or make a paste from biological (enzyme) detergent and warm water and rub on to both sides of wet fabric. Rinse and launder as above.

On non-washable fabrics, dab with lukewarm water and then treat with dry-cleaning spot cleaner.

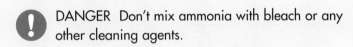

EXCREMENT **Protein**

These brown stains are not to be confused with chocolate. If in doubt, identify by smell.

Removal
Easy

DON'T use hot water, tumble dry or iron until the stain has been removed completely – heat sets excrement stains.

 Clear up as much excess excrement as possible with kitchen towels. Rinse immediately under cold running water or soak in cold water, gently agitating the back of the fabric against itself.

Bleach whites and baby clothes with lemon juice, then leave in the sun to dry.

On carpets and upholstery, spray or sponge with soda water, saturating the area. Keep blotting and reapplying soda water until the stain has lifted. If the stain persists, squirt a tiny amount of shaving cream over it and brush gently into the fibres with an old toothbrush. Wipe away excess foam with a clean dry cloth and blot with a sponge dipped in cold water.

On non-washable fabrics, dilute 1 teaspoon ammonia in 1 cup lukewarm water, colour test, then sponge over the stain. If the stain persists, dry clean.

 Gently agitate the back of the fabric against itself in cold water with biological (enzyme) detergent or pre-soak, then leave to soak overnight. If the stain persists, cover both sides with biological (enzyme) liquid detergent or stain stick and launder in warm water.

On carpets and upholstery, clean up the excess as above. Make a solution from warm water, biological (enzyme) detergent and a little disinfectant and sponge over repeatedly. Treat remaining traces with soda water as above. Add a little antiseptic to the final rinse.

EYELINER/PENCIL/SHADOW

Combination

Can be any colour but often appear as black or brown marks on towels and pillowcases.

Removal
Moderate

 Sponge with warm water, then rub washing-up liquid into the stain and gently agitate the back of the fabric against itself or scrub the back of the stain gently with a toothbrush. Launder. Repeat as necessary.

Alternatively, spot treat with methylated spirits, blotting at the back (see page 7). Rinse and launder.

On non-washable fabrics, carpets and upholstery, dilute 1 part ammonia in 3 parts cold water and colour test. Dab on to the carpet surface or back of the stain, leave for 5 minutes and rinse. If any remains, squirt on a tiny amount of shaving cream and brush gently into the fibres with an old toothbrush. Wipe away excess foam with a clean dry cloth and blot with a sponge dipped in cold water. Take non-colourfast clothing to the dry cleaner.

 Soak in warm water with biological (enzyme) detergent or pre-soak for 30 minutes. Launder with biological (enzyme) detergent in the hottest water that is safe for the fabric.

If the stain persists, soak in all-fabric bleach solution for 15 minutes, rinse and launder. If the stain still remains, and the fabric can take it, soak in chlorine bleach solution for 15 minutes, rinse and launder.

Alternatively, spot treat with grease-solvent stain remover, blotting at the back of the stain. Rinse thoroughly from the fabric, then air dry before laundering with biological (enzyme) detergent.

FACE CREAM **Greasy**

Face and hand creams are vegetable or petroleum based and stains are relatively easy to remove, but anything other than a tiny spot will spread readily. The stains can be any skin-tone colour from beige to dark brown.

Removal
Moderate

 Scrape off as much excess face cream as possible with a spoon or old credit card, working from the outside of the stain inwards to avoid spreading it any further.

Dampen with the hottest water that is safe. Rub liquid detergent into the stain, and feather with an old toothbrush, working in towards the centre of the stain.

On carpets and upholstery, scrape off the excess as above and sprinkle with bicarbonate of soda, cornflour or talcum powder. Leave for several hours, then vacuum. If it persists, squirt over a tiny amount of shaving cream and brush gently into the fibres with an old toothbrush. Wipe away excess foam with a clean dry cloth and blot with a sponge dipped in cold water.

 Spot treat with grease-solvent stain remover, dabbing at the back of the stain (see page 7). Rinse thoroughly from the fabric, then air dry and launder.

If the stain persists, rub in biological (enzyme) liquid detergent and launder with biological (enzyme) detergent in the hottest water that is safe for the fabric.

FACE POWDER Combination

These powder stains come in all skin-tone colours.

Removal
Moderate

 Brush off any excess powder. Rinse in cold water, gently agitating the back of the fabric against itself. Sponge with warm water and apply washing-up liquid or liquid detergent to both sides of the stain. Gently agitate the back of the fabric against itself, then rinse thoroughly. Repeat as necessary. This method also works with non-gel shampoo, bar soap or toothpaste.

Alternatively, sprinkle with borax, work into the back of the stain and rinse.

On carpets and upholstery, brush off the excess as above. Dilute 1 tablespoon borax in 500 ml (1 pint) warm water. Sponge on to the stain, alternating with clean, warm water as the stain is removed.

For old stains, cover the back of the stain with bicarbonate of soda and brush in gently with a damp nailbrush or toothbrush. Rinse thoroughly.

 Brush off the excess as above, then soak in biological (enzyme) pre-soak for 30 minutes. Rinse thoroughly. Rub biological (enzyme) liquid detergent into both sides, then launder with biological (enzyme) detergent in the hottest water that is safe for the fabric.

If the stain persists, soak in all-fabric bleach solution for 15 minutes, rinse and launder. If the stain still remains, and the fabric can take it, soak in chlorine bleach solution for 15 minutes, rinse and launder.

FELT-TIP, PERMANENT Dye

Permanent felt-tip markers are made to be irremovable. If you don't know if the marker is washable or permanent, treat as washable first (see opposite). If the stain is on a valuable piece of clothing, washable or not, don't risk making it worse – dry clean.

Removal
Difficult

 Add 4 tablespoons ammonia to 1 litre (2 pints) warm soapy water. Soak for 1 hour and rinse thoroughly.

Alternatively, spot treat with rubbing alcohol or turpentine (see page 7). Take care to keep the mark contained, always working towards the centre of the stain with a light, feathering movement. Rinse thoroughly from the fabric and air dry, then launder.

If the stain persists, rub a weak solution of washing-up liquid and water into both sides of the stain. Leave this on and launder in the hottest water that is safe for the fabric.

Colour test, then spot treat the back of the stain with acetone – don't use acetone on acetate fabrics. Rinse the fabric thoroughly.

Rub biological (enzyme) detergent into both sides of the stain and launder with biological (enzyme) detergent in the hottest water that is safe for the fabric.

If the stain persists, soak in all-fabric bleach solution for 15 minutes, rinse and launder. If the stain remains, and the fabric can take it, soak in chlorine bleach solution for 15 minutes, rinse and launder.

On table surfaces, wipe with nail varnish remover or methylated spirits. Rinse and repeat as necessary.

FELT-TIP, WASHABLE Tannin

These stains come in a multitude of colours. Washable should mean what it says: if, after laundering, the mark hasn't washed out at all, the ink might be of the permanent kind.

Removal
Easy

DON'T use any kind of soap – soap sets felt-tip stains.

Soaking in milk works really well. You don't have to fill a bucket with milk – just make sure the whole of the stained area is saturated and leave for several hours. Rinse thoroughly and launder.

Alternatively, spot treat with rubbing alcohol, blotting at the back of the stain (see page 7). Rinse the fabric thoroughly.

If you don't have any rubbing alcohol, try hairspray – be sure to use a non-oily variety, as the oil content could create a new stain.

On carpets and upholstery, spray or sponge with soda water, saturating the area. Keep blotting and reapplying soda water until the stain has lifted. If the stain persists, apply a weak solution of washing-up liquid and water and blot. Repeat as necessary.

On non-washable fabrics, if you are sure the ink is washable and not permanent, spot treat with dry-cleaning solvent, dabbing at the back of the fabric.

If you are uncertain as to whether the stain is washable or permanent, home treatment will only make things worse, so take to the dry cleaner for professional spot cleaning.

FLOOR POLISH, SOLVENT BASED Combination

Floor polish leaves a strong-smelling, waxy, greasy stain.

Removal
Moderate

 Scrape off as much excess polish as possible with a spoon or old credit card. Rub liquid detergent into both sides of the stain and then scrub in the hottest water that is safe for the fabric.

If the stain persists, colour test with a dab of white vinegar, then make a paste from white vinegar and cornflour, apply to the stain and leave to dry in. Launder in the hottest water that is safe for the fabric.

This solution can also be used on carpets and upholstery. Apply, leave to dry, then vacuum off.

 Scrape off excess polish as above, then wet both sides with cool water, apply stain stick and launder.

Alternatively, spot treat with dry-cleaning solvent, dabbing at the back of the stain (see page 7). Rinse thoroughly from the fabric and air dry, then launder.

If traces of the stain remain, rub biological (enzyme) liquid detergent into both sides of the stain. Leave this on and launder with biological (enzyme) detergent in the hottest water that is safe for the fabric.

If the stain persists, soak in all-fabric bleach solution for 15 minutes, rinse and launder. If the stain still remains, and the fabric can take it, soak in chlorine bleach solution for 15 minutes, rinse and launder.

FLOOR POLISH, WATER BASED Tannin

Not as dense as solvent-based, water-based polish. Leaves purple, pink or yellowish stains.

Removal
Easy

DON'T use any kind of soap – soap sets polish stains.

 Scrape off as much excess polish as possible with a spoon or old credit card. Rub liquid detergent into both sides of the stain and then scrub in the hottest water that is safe for the fabric.

 Scrape off excess polish as above, then wet both sides of the stain with cool water and apply stain stick. Leave this on and launder with biological (enzyme) detergent in the hottest water that is safe for the fabric.

Alternatively, soak in warm water with biological (enzyme) pre-soak for 30 minutes before laundering with biological (enzyme) detergent.

On carpets and upholstery, make a paste from equal parts bicarbonate of soda and salt mixed with a few drops of cold water. Spread over the stain and leave to dry for 30 minutes, then vacuum off.

FLOOR WAX **Combination**

Floor wax leaves a strong-smelling, waxy, greasy stain.

Removal
Moderate

Scrape off as much excess polish as possible with a spoon or old credit card. Rub liquid detergent into both sides of the stain and then scrub in the hottest water that is safe for the fabric.

If the stain persists, colour test with a dab of white vinegar, then make a paste from white vinegar and cornflour, apply to the stain and leave to dry in. Launder in the hottest water that is safe for the fabric.

On carpets and upholstery, scrape off excess wax as above and then sprinkle with cornflour, bicarbonate of soda or talcum powder. Leave for several hours – overnight if possible – then vacuum. If the stain persists, squirt a tiny amount of shaving cream over the stain and brush gently into the fibres with an old toothbrush. Wipe away excess foam with a clean dry cloth and blot with a sponge dipped in cold water.

Scrape off excess wax as above and then wet both sides of the stain with cool water, apply stain stick and launder as usual.

Alternatively, spot treat with dry-cleaning solvent, dabbing at the back of the stain (see page 7). Rinse the solvent thoroughly from the fabric and air dry before laundering.

If traces of the stain remain, rub biological (enzyme) liquid detergent into both sides of the stain. Leave this on and launder with biological (enzyme) detergent in the hottest water that is safe for the fabric.

If the stain persists, soak the fabric in all-fabric bleach solution for 15 minutes, rinse and then launder as usual. If the stain still remains, and the fabric can take it, soak in chlorine bleach solution for 15 minutes, rinse and launder.

FOOD COLOURINGS Dye

These include brightly coloured stains from ice lollies, ice pops, fruit squashes and some juices.

Removal
Moderate

DON'T use hot water, tumble dry or iron until the stain has been removed completely – heat sets food colouring stains.

 Soak immediately with soda water. Reapply and dab with kitchen towels or an absorbent white cloth.

If you don't have any soda water, stretch the fabric tight and hold the back under cold running water.

If the stain persists, mix 1 tablespoon ammonia in 1 cup water, colour test and then spot treat, dabbing at the back of the stain (see page 7). Cover the front with salt and work this into the fabric. Leave for 1 hour, then brush away the salt. Repeat as necessary.

For really stubborn stains, spot treat with equal parts methylated spirits and ammonia.

 Apply red wine pre-treatment stain remover to red, orange and purple stains as directed, rinse and launder.

Alternatively, soak immediately in all-fabric bleach solution for 15 minutes, rinse and launder. If the stain persists, and the fabric can take it, soak in chlorine bleach solution for 15 minutes, rinse and launder.

FOUNDATION MAKE-UP Combination

Liquid or pan stick comes in all skin tone colours and leaves greasy pink or brown stains.

Removal
Moderate

Liquid foundation contains less grease and so is not as difficult to remove as concentrated pan stick.

 Sponge the stain with warm water and apply washing-up liquid or liquid detergent to both sides. Gently agitate the back of the fabric against itself, then rinse thoroughly. Repeat as necessary. You can also use non-gel shampoo, bar soap or toothpaste.

Alternatively, sprinkle with borax and work into back of the stain. Rinse.

For really oily foundations and pan sticks, cover the back with bicarbonate of soda and brush in gently with a damp nailbrush or toothbrush. Rinse thoroughly.

On carpets and upholstery, scrape off as much excess foundation as possible with a spoon or old credit card. Dilute 1 tablespoon borax in 500 ml (1 pint) warm water. Sponge on to the stain, alternating with clean warm water as the stain is removed.

If the stain persists, squirt on a tiny amount of shaving cream and brush gently into the fibres with an old toothbrush. Wipe away excess foam with a clean dry cloth and blot with a sponge dipped in cold water.

Soak in biological (enzyme) pre-soak for 30 minutes and rinse thoroughly. Rub biological (enzyme) liquid detergent into both sides of the stain and launder with biological (enzyme) detergent in the hottest water that is safe for the fabric.

If the stain persists, soak in all-fabric bleach solution for 15 minutes, rinse and launder. If the stain still remains, and the fabric can take it, soak in chlorine bleach solution for 15 minutes, rinse and launder.

FRUIT AND FRUIT JUICE Tannin

These stains can usually be identified by smell, if not colour.

Removal
Moderate

DON'T use any kind of soap – soap sets fruit stains.

 If still wet, stretch the fabric right side down over a sink, bowl or saucepan, securing with clothes pegs or an elastic band. Pour through the hottest water that is safe for the fabric from the back of the stain, from as high as possible without danger of splashing.

For dry stains, first soak in a 50/50 warm water/glycerine mixture for 1 hour. This works particularly well for woollens. If the stain is stubborn, colour test and sponge on a 50/50 white vinegar/water mixture, then rinse and leave to dry in the sun.

Sponge non-washable fabrics with cold water. If the stain persists, mix 3 parts borax to 1 part water and spread the paste on the stain.

On carpets, soak with soda water and rinse. Alternatively, mix a paste of 3 parts borax to 1 part water and rub into the stained area. Leave to dry and then vacuum off.

 Rub the back of the stain with biological (enzyme) liquid detergent, then soak in lukewarm water and biological (enzyme) detergent for 30 minutes. If the stain persists, soak the fabric for 15 minutes in all-fabric bleach solution.

Sponge non-washable fabrics with cold water before applying an appropriate pre-treatment product.

You can get rid of fruit stains on fingers with nail polish remover.

On carpets and upholstery, sponge with cold water before applying an enzyme stain remover. Rinse and clean with carpet or upholstery shampoo.

GELATINE Special

Gelatine stains are yellowish, greasy-looking stains, but should not be treated as such.

Removal
Moderate

DON'T use hot water, tumble dry or iron until the stain has been removed completely – heat sets gelatine stains.

 Scrape off as much excess gelatine as possible with a spoon or blunt knife, then spray or sponge with soda water. Keep blotting and reapplying soda water until the stain has lifted. If the stain persists, dilute a non-bleach detergent in cold water and apply in the same way.

If the stain still remains, soak in a solution of 2 tablespoons borax to 500 ml (1 pint) water for 1 hour and then launder. For woollens, spot treat the back of the stain with borax solution (see page 7).

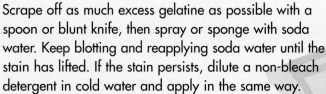 Scrape off the excess and treat with soda water as above. If the stain persists, soak in lukewarm water with biological (enzyme) detergent or pre-soak.

Don't launder until most of the stain is gone. Launder with biological (enzyme) liquid detergent in warm water.

GLUE Special

White glue and school paste dry with a white filmy crust. Other glues solidify into yellowish stains.

Removal
Easy to impossible, depending on the type of glue

 For white glue and school paste, spot treat the back of the stain with soda water (see page 7) or soak the fabric immediately in cold water. Gently agitate the back of the fabric against itself or hold the back of the stain under cold running water and let it run through for 5 minutes or until the stain disappears.

On carpets and upholstery, spray or sponge with soda water, saturating the area. Keep blotting and reapplying soda water until the stain has lifted.

For contact adhesive, don't allow it to set but rinse immediately in cool water.

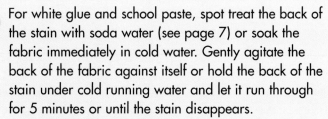 Treat glues other than white glue and school paste with an appropriate glue solvent. Don't use strong solvents on foam-backed carpets as this could result in permanent damage to the backing. It may be possible to remove hardened glue by carefully snipping away the top fibres with very sharp, fine scissors.

For clear glue, colour test and then spot treat with an appropriate solvent. Rinse thoroughly before laundering with biological (enzyme) detergent. Use white spirit on acetates and triacetates.

Don't allow latex adhesive to set – rinse immediately in cool water. If the glue has already set, spot treat with a specialist solvent or paintbrush cleaner. Rinse the solvent thoroughly from the fabric and air dry before laundering.

Epoxy adhesive, a tough and flexible glue used mainly for marine and industrial purposes, is impossible to remove once set. Rinse immediately in cool water. If any residue remains, spot treat with methylated spirits or paint thinner. Rinse and launder.

For animal- or fish-based glue, rinse in cool water. If the stain persists, soak in biological (enzyme) detergent or pre-soak for 30 minutes and then launder with biological (enzyme) detergent. Alternatively, colour test and dab on ammonia. Don't use neat ammonia on woollens or silk: dilute it 50/50 with cool water.

Superglue is not a super stainer. If it does stain, take to the dry cleaner as soon as possible. On carpets and upholstery, dab on non-oily nail varnish. If this doesn't work, use a specialist superglue remover.

GRASS Special

Grass leaves green marks, often mixed with mud.

Removal
Moderate

DON'T use detergent directly on grass stains – detergent sets grass stains.

 Colour test, then soak in white vinegar. On some fabrics, this will work instantly; others will need soaking for up to 2 hours. For non-colourfast fabrics, dilute the vinegar 50/50 with warm water.

Spot treat small stains with non-gel toothpaste or white vinegar. Rinse and repeat as necessary.

For stubborn stains, spot treat with methylated spirits. Rinse and launder. Don't use methylated spirits on acetates or wool.

On carpets and upholstery, make a paste from equal parts salt and cream of tartar plus a few drops of water. Leave to dry, then brush off.

On non-washable fabrics, spot treat with the same paste as above. If this doesn't work, dry clean.

 Soak in biological (enzyme) pre-soak for 30 minutes or dampen with cool water and apply stain stick or biological (enzyme) liquid detergent. Launder with biological (enzyme) detergent in warm water. Soak stubborn stains in all-fabric bleach for 15 minutes.

GRAVY **Combination**

Gravy leaves thick, greasy, brown stains.

Removal
Moderate

 Treat the protein part of the stain first. Scrape or blot off as much excess gravy as possible with a spoon, blunt knife or kitchen towels, then spot treat with soda water or lukewarm, soapy water, dabbing at the back of the stain (see page 7). Rinse under cold running water. If gravy spills on a white tablecloth during a meal, a piece of white bread soaked in soda water or cool water will act as a sponge.

Don't launder until most of the stain has been removed. Make a paste from powdered detergent and water and rub into both sides of stain, then launder in warm water.

If the stain persists, colour test and then spot treat with ammonia, dabbing at the back of the stain.

 Scrape or blot off excess gravy as above. Spot treat with a specialist solvent or stain stick, rinse and leave to air dry, then launder with biological (enzyme) detergent.

If the stain persists, soak in all-fabric bleach solution for 15 minutes, rinse and launder. If the stain still remains, and the fabric can take it, soak in chlorine bleach solution for 15 minutes, rinse and launder.

For stubborn stains on carpets, dilute ½ cup 3 per cent hydrogen peroxide bleach (NOT hair bleach, see page 16) in 1 cup water. Colour test and then blot over the stain and leave for 1 hour. Rinse and repeat as necessary.

On non-washable fabrics, blot up excess gravy as above and take to the dry cleaner as soon as possible.

GREASE Greasy

Grease stains quickly penetrate the fibres of fabrics and carpets and are liable to spread if not treated carefully. The stain is likely to be deeper in colour at the centre, fading to a paler shade towards the edges.

Removal
Moderate

Grease stains left for longer than 24 hours on polyester, nylon or nylon/polyester blends will be very difficult to remove.

 Dab up as much excess grease as possible with kitchen towels or an absorbent white cloth. If it's a fatty grease stain that has hardened, scrape off the crust carefully with a blunt knife, working from the outside of the stain inwards to avoid spreading it. Sprinkle with bicarbonate of soda, cornflour or talcum powder and rub gently into the stain. Leave for 30 minutes to allow the powder to absorb the grease, then wipe off with a dry flannel facecloth. This method works on both washable and non-washable fabrics.

Alternatively, work a little washing-up liquid into both sides. Leave for 5 minutes before soaking in a bucket of water to which ½ cup washing-up liquid has been added. Leave for 30 minutes.

If the stain persists, mix bicarbonate of soda with a little cold water to make a thick paste, apply and leave until it has dried in completely, then brush off.

Whites can be soaked in warm water and washing soda or borax, 1 tablespoon to 1 pint water.

Launder in the hottest water that is safe for the fabric in a 50/50 detergent/bicarbonate of soda wash.

On carpets and upholstery, dab up excess grease and sprinkle with powder as above to absorb excess grease. Leave for several hours – overnight if possible – then vacuum. If the stain persists, squirt a tiny amount of shaving cream over the stain and brush gently into the fibres with an old toothbrush. Wipe away excess foam with a clean dry cloth and blot with a sponge dipped in cold water.

Greasy marks on wallpaper can be removed by making a paste from Fuller's earth and water and pasting over the stain. Leave to dry, then brush off.

 Dab up and sprinkle with powder as above to absorb excess grease, then spot treat with grease-solvent stain remover, feathering at the back of the stain (see page 7). Rinse the solvent thoroughly from the fabric and air dry before laundering.

Alternatively, rub biological (enzyme) liquid detergent into both sides of the stain. Leave this on and launder with biological (enzyme) detergent in the hottest water that is safe for the fabric.

GROUP, STAINS ON Combination

Black stains on tile grouting are usually a combination of mildew, mould and dirt.

Removal
Moderate to difficult – as grout is porous, it absorbs the cleaner without removing the stain. When re-tiling, treat grout with a protective coating available from builder's merchants or hardware stores. After showering, rub down the tiles with a towel.

 For light staining on white tiled areas, scrub on bicarbonate of soda with an old nailbrush or toothbrush and rinse. If the tiling or grouting is coloured, wear rubber gloves and make a paste from washing soda or borax and water. Scrub into the stains.

 For stubborn stains, make a paste from 3 per cent hydrogen peroxide bleach (NOT hair bleach, see page 16) and water. Paste on to the stains with an old knife or spoon. Leave for 15 minutes before rinsing.

Eco-friendly grout cleaners are available that don't contain phosphates, dyes, perfumes or fillers.

Alternatively, use a grout stainer, available from builder's merchants or hardware stores. Odourless and non-hazardous, its water-based acrylic coating will either restore or change the colour of existing grouting. It also protects grouting from future staining. It is suitable for all kinds of tiling except limestone and other porous tiles, stone and tumbled marble.

HAIR DYE Dye

Hair dye stains usually dry to dark brown, though they can be lighter or darker. Because of their very high dyeing fastness, these will probably never be removed.

Removal
Difficult – impossible if dried in

 For fresh stains on washable fabrics, soak immediately in cold water, then rub washing-up liquid into both sides and gently agitate the back of the fabric against itself. Colour test, then rub white vinegar into both sides and leave to soak for 2 hours. Launder.

For fresh stains on non-washable fabrics, rub in a little washing-up liquid with a cotton bud. If this doesn't work, dry clean as soon as possible.

Spot treat henna stains with ammonia (colour test first) or methylated spirits (see page 7). Rinse thoroughly and launder.

For stains on your skin after dyeing your hair, use a make-up remover wipe.

On carpets and upholstery, blot up as much dye as possible with kitchen towels. Add a small squirt of washing-up liquid to a cup of lukewarm water and dab on to the stain with an absorbent white cloth. Leave for 5 minutes and rinse. Repeat as necessary.

As a last resort on permanently damaged carpets and upholstery, carefully dab on 3 per cent hydrogen peroxide bleach with a cotton bud (NOT hair bleach, see page 16), to bleach out the colour of the stain completely. Then fill in with felt-tip pen.

Leave washable fabrics to soak overnight in warm water with a biological (enzyme) pre-soak. Soak whites and colourfast fabrics in chlorine bleach for 15 minutes, then launder.

HAND LOTION **Greasy**

A liquid with oils designed to penetrate and soften the skin, hand lotion leaves behind thick, greasy stains.

Removal
Moderate

Scrape off and dab up as much excess lotion as possible with a spoon or old credit card and kitchen towels or an absorbent white cloth. Work from the outside of the stain inwards to avoid spreading it any further. Sprinkle with bicarbonate of soda, cornflour or talcum powder and rub gently into the stain. Leave for 30 minutes to allow the powder to absorb the lotion, then wipe off with a dry flannel facecloth. This method works on both washable and non-washable fabrics.

Alternatively, work a little washing-up liquid into both sides of the stain. Leave for 5 minutes, then soak in a bucket of water to which ½ cup washing-up liquid has been added. Leave for 30 minutes.

Launder in the hottest water that is safe for the fabric in a 50/50 detergent/bicarbonate of soda wash.

On carpets and upholstery, dab up and sprinkle on powder as above to absorb excess lotion. Leave for several hours – overnight if possible – then vacuum. If the stain persists, squirt over a tiny amount of shaving cream and brush gently into the fibres with an old toothbrush. Wipe away excess foam with a clean dry cloth and blot with a sponge dipped in cold water.

Spot treat with grease-solvent stain remover (see page 7). Rinse thoroughly from the fabric and air dry before laundering with biological (enzyme) detergent in the hottest water that is safe for the fabric.

Treat stubborn stains on carpets and upholstery with dry-cleaning solvent. Apply it carefully, avoiding the carpet backing as the fluid may cause permanent damage, and sponge off with a clean, damp cloth.

HEEL MARKS Special

Rubber heels and soles can leave nasty black marks on floors, stone being especially vulnerable. Always test any stain-removal procedure on a hidden area of the floor first.

Removal
Moderate

Marks left untreated for any longer than a week will be very difficult to remove.

DON'T use a water-based cleaner, or a cleaner that has to be rinsed off, on wood floors.

 Try rubbing out the marks with a pencil eraser.
On waxed floors, rub in turpentine. This will remove any wax coating, so the area will need to be re-waxed.

 Anything but a very fine scouring powder may leave scratch marks. If you do use it, rub very lightly.
On non-waxed floors, use a specialist solvent-based cleaning product. Apply directly to the stain and dab at the mark with a non-abrasive nylon pad. Rinse well.
Alternatively, rub with very fine steel wool and floor detergent. Wipe dry and apply polish immediately. Stubborn old marks can be removed manually with a buffer-pad tool attachment. Consult a professional.
On stone floors, mix equal parts white spirit and warm water with a squirt of washing-up liquid. Rub on the stain, working from the outside inwards with your fingertip inside a cloth or a cotton bud. Rinse.

HONEY Tannin

Pale yellow sticky stains. Honey, marmalade, jam and jelly stains can all be treated in the same way.

Removal
Easy, if treated immediately. If you cannot treat stains straight away, sprinkle with salt.

DON'T use soap of any kind – soap sets honey, marmalade, jam and jelly stains.

 Scrape off as much excess honey as possible with a spoon or old credit card, working from the outside of the stain inwards. Rinse in cold water.
Rub liquid detergent into both sides and leave for 5 minutes. Stretch the fabric right side down over a sink, bowl or saucepan, securing with clothes pegs or an elastic band. Pour through the hottest water that is safe for the fabric from the back, from as high as possible without danger of splashing.
For old, stubborn stains, mix equal parts white vinegar and warm water, colour test, then sponge on and leave to dry in the sun. Repeat as necessary. Or, rub the back with glycerine, leave for 1 hour and rinse.
On non-washable fabrics, scrape off excess honey as above, dab with cold water and apply a little washing-up liquid. Dab with cool water. Or, sprinkle with borax, rub in gently and leave for 5 minutes, then dab with cool water. If this doesn't work, dry clean.
On carpets and upholstery, scrape off excess honey as above, then squirt over a tiny amount of shaving

cream and brush gently into the fibres with an old toothbrush. Wipe away excess foam with a clean dry cloth and blot with a sponge dipped in cold water.

 Scrape off excess honey as above. Apply stain stick to both sides, then launder with biological (enzyme) detergent in the hottest water that is safe for the fabric.

For old, stubborn stains, mix 1 part 3 per cent hydrogen peroxide bleach (NOT hair bleach, see page 16) with 6 parts water. Colour test and then soak for 15 minutes. Rinse and launder.

HUMMUS **Combination**

These pale brown stains have both an olive-oil grease element and a protein chickpea element.

Removal
Easy

 Scrape off as much excess hummus as possible with a spoon or old credit card, working from the outside of the stain inwards. Rinse in cold water.

Rub liquid detergent into both sides of the stain and leave for 5 minutes. Stretch the fabric right side down over a sink, bowl or saucepan, securing with clothes pegs or an elastic band. Pour through the hottest water that is safe for the fabric from the back of the stain, from as high as possible without danger of splashing.

For old, stubborn stains, mix equal parts white vinegar and warm water, colour test, then sponge on and leave to dry in the sun. Alternatively, rub the back of the stain with glycerine, leave for 1 hour and rinse.

On non-washable fabrics, scrape off excess as above, dab with cold water and apply a little washing-up liquid. Dab with cool water, taking care not to spread the stain. Or, sprinkle with borax, rub in gently and leave for 5 minutes, then dab with cool water. If this doesn't work, dry clean as soon as possible.

On carpets and upholstery, scrape off excess as above, then squirt over a tiny amount of shaving cream and brush gently into the fibres with an old toothbrush. Wipe away excess foam with a clean dry cloth and blot with a sponge dipped in cold water.

 Scrape off excess hummus as above. Apply stain stick to both sides of the stain, leave this on and launder with biological (enzyme) detergent in the hottest water that is safe for the fabric.

ICE CREAM Combination

Varying in colour from cream to chocolate brown, this combination of dairy products and sugar quickly melts into the fibres of clothing, carpets and upholstery, causing spectacular stains.

Removal
Easy to moderate

Ice-cream stains containing chocolate or fruits are combination stains and will be slightly more difficult to remove. Treat the protein part of the stain first, as here, then look up the appropriate flavouring to treat the chocolate or fruit stain.

DON'T use hot water, tumble dry or iron until the stain has been removed completely – heat sets ice-cream stains.

 Scrape off as much excess ice cream as possible with a spoon or old credit card, working from the outside of the stain inwards to avoid spreading it further, and soak as soon as possible in cold water. If the stain occurs away from home, dab the back of it immediately with cold water or, if possible, soda water.

Carpets and upholstery can be treated in the same way, or with washing-up liquid. Squirt a little directly on to the stain and sponge off with lukewarm water.

For stubborn, dried-in stains, dilute 1 tablespoon borax in 500 ml (1 pint) warm water. Dab over with a clean cloth or sponge and rinse. Repeat as necessary.

 Soak in a biological (enzyme) pre-soak in lukewarm water for 30 minutes. If the stain persists, spot treat with stain stick on both sides of the stain (see page 7). Leave this on and launder with biological (enzyme) detergent in warm water.

On non-washable fabrics, anything other than spot stains are best taken to the dry cleaner as soon as possible. For small marks, dissolve biological (enzyme) detergent in lukewarm water and spot treat the back of the stain, or use a grease-solvent stain remover.

ICE LOLLY Tannin

These very common stains come in a variety of colours, from cola-brown to cherry-pink.

Removal
Moderate

Make sure every trace of the spill is removed as quickly as possible. Some stains containing sugar are invisible when they dry but turn yellow with heat or age and are then impossible to remove.

 Rinse immediately in cold water. Rub washing-up liquid into the back of the stain, gently agitating the back of the fabric against itself. Rinse and launder.

If the stain has dried in, apply glycerine to the back of it and leave for 30 minutes before treating with washing-up liquid as above.

On non-washable fabrics, sponge with cold water, then spot treat with methylated spirits (see page 7).

 Rinse immediately in cold water. Rub biological (enzyme) liquid detergent into the back of the stain and gently agitate the back of the fabric against itself. Launder with biological (enzyme) detergent in the hottest water that is safe for the fabric.

DON'T use any kind of soap –
soap sets ice lolly stains.

If the stain persists, apply stain stick to both sides of the fabric and launder again.

On carpets and upholstery, blot up as much excess ice lolly as possible with kitchen towels or an absorbent cloth. Dilute biological (enzyme) liquid detergent in cold water and agitate to froth it up. Sponge over the stained area, then sponge off with cold water. Repeat until as much of the stain as possible has been removed. If any remains, treat with carpet stain remover.

INK, INDELIBLE/PERMANENT Dye

Ink leaves prominent, usually black or blue marks. Some types of ink will be set by laundering, so don't launder until you have tried to remove the stain first.

Removal
Difficult

Indelible ink is manufactured to be irremovable. Dried ink is much harder to remove than ink that is still wet.

 If the mark is still fresh, try holding the back of the stain under a cold water tap and letting the force of the water remove the pigments. Spot treat with methylated spirits (see page 7), rinse and launder. Don't use meths on acetate or triacetate fabrics.

Alternatively, add 4 tablespoons ammonia to a bowl of warm water. Colour test, then leave to soak for 4–8 hours or overnight if possible. Rinse thoroughly.

On tough surfaces, indelible ink may come off by rubbing with a damp pumice stone.

To remove ink stains from fingers, dip a soft nailbrush in white vinegar, then salt and brush gently.

 If the flushing method above has had some impact on the stain, follow up by spot treating with a dry-cleaning solvent. The ink manufacturer may recommend a particular solvent. Rinse the solvent thoroughly from the fabric and air dry before laundering. If the stain persists, rub in biological (enzyme) liquid detergent. Leave this on and launder with biological (enzyme) detergent in the hottest water that is safe for the fabric.

On wood, apply a tiny amount of wood bleach using a cotton bud and wipe off immediately. Repeat as necessary. Restore the colour with shoe polish or a specialist wood-treatment colour stick and polish up.

INK, WASHABLE Tannin

Washable should mean what it says, but it is safer to treat these stains – which are usually black or blue – first, rather than putting them straight in the wash.

Removal
Easy

DON'T use any kind of soap – soap sets ink stains.

 Soaking in milk works really well. You don't have to fill a bucket with milk – just make sure the whole of the stained area is saturated and leave for 2 hours. Rinse thoroughly and launder.

Alternatively, spot treat the back of the stain with methylated spirits (see page 7). Rinse thoroughly. If you don't have any meths, you could try hairspray, but be sure to use a non-oily type or the oil content will create a new stain.

On carpets and upholstery, spray or sponge with soda water, saturating the area. Keep blotting and reapplying soda water until the stain has lifted. If the stain persists, apply a weak solution of washing-up liquid and water to the stained area and blot. Repeat as necessary.

 Apply biological (enzyme) liquid detergent to both sides of the stain and launder with biological (enzyme) detergent as usual.

On non-washable fabrics, if you are sure the ink is washable and not permanent, sponge with a dry-cleaning spot treatment. If you are uncertain, home treatment with make things worse, so take to the dry cleaner for professional spot cleaning.

IODINE Chemical

Iodine stains are yellow or brown on unstarched fabrics; black or deep blue on starched fabrics.

Removal
Easy to moderate

 Fresh stains are easy to remove. Dampen the stain with water and leave in the sun or over a radiator. Alternatively, spray the stained area with warm water, then place face down on an ironing board and use the jet steam setting on a steam iron to blast out the stain.

Another method is to hold the back of the stain under a cool running tap or soak in mild detergent in cool water for several hours.

A further method is to dilute 1 tablespoon ammonia in 1 cup warm water; in a separate cup, mix 2 parts warm water to 1 part white vinegar. Colour test, then spot treat with ammonia solution (see page 7). Repeat with the vinegar solution. Then blot the stain with a warm solution of mild detergent and rinse. Repeat the whole process as necessary.

On linen, rub the stain with a slice of lemon or lime.

 Soak whites in a colour-remover product.

Alternatively, spot treat with sodium thiosulphate crystals (available from pharmacies). Rinse thoroughly and launder.

KETCHUP Combination

Ketchup is a tomato-based stain, like barbeque sauce and tomato sauce (see pages 34 and 118). It is often mistaken for blood.

Removal
Easy, but moderate if the stain has set

 Rinse as soon as possible under cold running water, gently agitating the back of the fabric against itself and letting the water run through. Colour test and then dab white vinegar all over the back of the stain and rinse again. Repeat several times.

Work liquid detergent into the back of the stain and launder in the hottest water that is safe for the fabric.

Alternatively, rub glycerine into the back of the stain and leave to soak in warm, soapy water for 1 hour.

 Rinse as soon as possible under cold running water as above. Spot treat with red-wine solvent stain remover (see page 7). Rinse the solvent thoroughly from the fabric and air dry before laundering. If traces of the stain remain, rub biological (enzyme) liquid detergent into both sides of the stain. Leave this on and launder with biological (enzyme) detergent in the hottest water that is safe for the fabric.

If the stain persists, soak in all-fabric bleach solution for 15 minutes, rinse and launder. If the stain still remains, and the fabric can take it, soak in chlorine bleach solution for 15 minutes, rinse and launder.

LARD Greasy

Lard leaves a fast-penetrating, white greasy stain – melted lard will be absorbed into the fabric even faster.

Removal
Moderate

 Scrape off as much excess lard as possible immediately with a spoon or blunt knife, working from the outside of the stain inwards. Apply liquid detergent to the back and leave for 5 minutes, then launder.

On carpets and upholstery, cover the stain with bicarbonate of soda, cornflour or talcum powder. Leave for several hours – overnight if possible – then vacuum. Repeat as necessary. If the stain persists, squirt a tiny amount of shaving cream over it and brush gently into the fibres with an old toothbrush. Wipe away excess foam with a clean dry cloth and blot with a sponge dipped in cold water.

 Scrape off excess lard as above, then spot treat with grease-solvent stain remover (see page 7). Rinse thoroughly from the fabric and air dry, then launder. If the stain persists, rub in biological (enzyme) liquid detergent, then launder with biological (enzyme) detergent in the hottest water that is safe for the fabric.

On carpets and upholstery, scrape off excess lard as above and then treat with dry carpet cleaner.

LEAF STAINS Organic

These organic, mildew-like stains can appear on any exterior surface, such as roofs and decking areas.

Removal
Easy with the right product, though some areas (such as swimming pool linings) are much more troublesome

 Brush off excess dirt. Dilute a little washing-up liquid in a bucket of warm water, scrub on and rinse off.

 Brush off excess dirt. Mix 3 parts all-fabric bleach with 1 part water and add a few drops of washing-up liquid. Scrub on, leave for 15 minutes and rinse.

Rot mould and mildew stain removers are available from boat suppliers and are safe to use on fibreglass, fabrics, canvas, plastic, carpets, wood and painted surfaces. Dilute in water as directed.

For really stubborn stains, use a strong toilet-bowl cleaner containing hydrochloric acid. Apply as directed and rinse thoroughly.

 DANGER Handle with care and follow all safety instructions exactly.

LIME Organic

These are the rust-like stains you see in toilet bowls and on kitchen appliances, saucepans and glassware, known as limescale. They are caused by a mineral build-up in hard water.

Removal
Easy

 Empty a bottle of white vinegar into the toilet bowl and leave overnight. Add a cupful once a week or so, and build-up will never be a problem again. If you are to be away from home for any length of time, empty a bottle of white vinegar into the toilet before you go.

For limescale deposits above the waterline, soak kitchen towels in white vinegar and use to cover the stained area. Keep moist with more vinegar. Rinse.

For small stains on glass jars, taps and so on, rub vinegar into the stain using an absorbent white cloth.

 Sprinkle the stain with biological (enzyme) detergent powder and scrub in with a little water. Rinse.

If this doesn't work, use a 100 per cent bio-degradable limescale-removal spray. Leave to soak for 5 minutes on light stains, 30 minutes on heavy stains. Wipe with a thick cloth or sponge and rinse well.

For large, stubborn stains, use a combined water spot, rust and hard mineral-deposit remover.

LINSEED OIL Greasy

Linseed oil is often used for sealing unglazed terracotta tiled floors. When it dries out, it can leave a sticky, gel-like residue that attracts dirt and dust, making it difficult to clean.

Removal
Moderate

 Dab up as much excess oil as possible with kitchen towels or an absorbent white cloth, then sprinkle with bicarbonate of soda, cornflour or talcum powder and rub gently into the stain. Leave for 30 minutes, then wipe off with a dry flannel facecloth. This method works on both washable and non-washable fabrics.

Alternatively, work a little washing-up liquid into both sides. Leave for 5 minutes before soaking in a bucket of water to which ½ cup washing-up liquid has been added. Leave for 30 minutes.

Launder in the hottest water that is safe for the fabric in a 50/50 detergent/bicarbonate of soda wash.

On carpets and upholstery, dab off and sprinkle with powder as above. Leave overnight, then vacuum.

 Dab up and sprinkle with powder as above. Spot treat with grease-solvent stain remover (see page 7). Rinse thoroughly from the fabric and air dry, then launder.

LIPSTICK Combination

These waxy, greasy marks vary in colour and intensity from deep red to shiny gold.

Removal
Moderate

Lipstick stains spread easily, so always work from the outside of the mark inwards.

 Scrape off as much excess lipstick as possible with a spoon or blunt knife. Sponge warm water on to the stain, then apply non-gel white toothpaste, washing-up liquid or bar soap. Rub into the stain, gently agitating the back of the fabric against itself, or scrub the back of the stain gently with an old toothbrush. Launder.

Alternatively, spot treat with methylated spirits (see page 7). Rinse and launder.

On non-washable fabrics, carpets and upholstery, dilute 1 part ammonia in 3 parts cold water and colour test. Dab on to the carpet surface or on to the back of the stain. Leave for 5 minutes, then rinse. Dry clean non-colourfast fabrics as soon as possible.

On silk, cover with masking tape and quickly rip off.

 Soak in warm water and biological (enzyme) detergent or pre-soak for 30 minutes. Launder with biological (enzyme) detergent in the hottest water that is safe for the fabric.

If the stain persists, soak in all-fabric bleach solution for 15 minutes, rinse and launder. If the stain still remains, and the fabric can take it, soak in chlorine bleach solution for 15 minutes, rinse and launder.

LUBRICATING GREASE Greasy

This is an oily brown liquid that stains into greasy brown blobs.

Removal
Moderate

Grease stains left longer than 24 hours on polyester, nylon or nylon/polyester blends will be very difficult to remove.

 Dab up as much excess grease as possible with kitchen towels or an absorbent white cloth, then sprinkle with bicarbonate of soda, cornflour or talcum powder and rub gently into the stain. Leave for 30 minutes, then wipe off with a dry flannel facecloth. This method works on both washable and non-washable fabrics.

Alternatively, work a little washing-up liquid into both sides. Leave for 5 minutes before soaking in a bucket of water to which ½ cup washing-up liquid has been added. Leave for 30 minutes.

Launder in the hottest water that is safe for the fabric in a 50/50 detergent/bicarbonate of soda wash.

For overalls and clothes covered in grease, drench in cola before putting into the washing machine.

On carpets and upholstery, dab off and sprinkle with powder as before. Leave for several hours – overnight if possible – then vacuum. If the stain persists, squirt a tiny amount of shaving cream over the stain and brush gently into the fibres with an old toothbrush. Wipe away excess foam with a clean dry cloth and blot with a sponge dipped in cold water.

 Dab and sprinkle with powder as before, then spot treat with a grease-stain solvent (see page 7). Rinse thoroughly from the fabric and air dry, then launder.

Alternatively, rub biological (enzyme) liquid detergent into both sides, then launder with biological (enzyme) detergent in the hottest water that is safe for the fabric. If the stain persists, repeat the process.

Sponge non-washable fabrics with dry-cleaning solvent. If the stain remains, take to the dry cleaner.

MARGARINE **Greasy**

Margarine leaves a fast-penetrating, fatty, yellowish stain – melted margarine is absorbed even more quickly.

Removal
Moderate

 Scrape off as much excess margarine as possible, then sprinkle with bicarbonate of soda, cornflour or talcum powder and rub gently into the stain. Leave for 30 minutes, then wipe off with a dry flannel facecloth. This works on washable and non-washable fabrics.

Alternatively, work a little washing-up liquid into both sides. Leave for 5 minutes before soaking in a bucket of water to which ½ cup washing-up liquid has been added. Leave for 30 minutes.

Launder in the hottest water that is safe for the fabric in a 50/50 detergent/bicarbonate of soda wash.

On carpets and upholstery, scrape off and sprinkle with powder as above. Leave overnight, then vacuum. If the stain persists, squirt on a tiny amount of shaving cream and brush gently into the fibres with an old toothbrush. Wipe away excess foam with a clean dry cloth and blot with a sponge dipped in cold water.

 Rub biological (enzyme) liquid detergent into both sides, then launder with biological (enzyme) detergent in the hottest water that is safe for the fabric.

On carpets and upholstery, scrape off and sprinkle with powder as above. Treat with dry carpet cleaner.

MARKER PEN Dye

These pens are manufactured to name-tag laundry and won't come out in a normal wash. There are both washable and non-washable types.

Removal
Moderate

 Rinse in cold water. If some ink starts to bleed, treat as washable. Rub the back of the stain with non-gel toothpaste and scrub gently with an old toothbrush.

If this doesn't work, spot treat with methylated spirits (see page 7) and rinse thoroughly. Work liquid detergent into both sides of the stain and launder in the hottest water that is safe for the fabric.

 Colour test and then spot treat with dye-solvent stain remover. Rinse the solvent thoroughly from the fabric and air dry before laundering. If traces of the stain remain, rub biological (enzyme) liquid detergent into both sides of the stain. Leave this on and launder with biological (enzyme) detergent in the hottest water that is safe for the fabric.

If the stain persists, soak in all-fabric bleach solution for 15 minutes, rinse and launder. If the stain still remains, and the fabric can take it, soak in chlorine bleach solution for 15 minutes, rinse and launder.

MASCARA Combination

These black or brown marks are often found on pillowcases and towels.

Removal
Moderate

 Sponge the stain with warm water, then rub washing-up liquid into the stain and agitate the back of the fabric against itself or scrub the back of the stain gently with a toothbrush. Launder. Repeat the process as necessary.

Alternatively, spot treat with methylated spirits, blotting at the back of the stain (see page 7). Rinse and launder.

On non-washable fabrics, carpets and upholstery, dilute 1 part ammonia in 3 parts cold water and colour test. Dab on to the carpet surface or the back of the stain, leave for 5 minutes and rinse. If any stain remains, squirt on a tiny amount of shaving cream and brush gently into the fibres with an old toothbrush. Wipe away excess foam with a clean dry cloth and blot with a sponge dipped in cold water. Take non-colourfast clothing to the dry cleaner as soon as possible.

Soak in warm water with biological (enzyme) detergent or pre-soak for 30 minutes. Launder with biological (enzyme) detergent in the hottest water that is safe for the fabric.

If the stain persists, soak in all-fabric bleach solution for 15 minutes, rinse and launder. If the stain still remains, and the fabric can take it, soak in chlorine bleach solution for 15 minutes, rinse and launder.

Alternatively, spot treat with grease-solvent stain remover, blotting at the back of the stain. Rinse the solvent thoroughly from the fabric and air dry before laundering with biological (enzyme) detergent.

MAYONNAISE *Greasy*

A mixture of egg yolks, oils and lemon juice, mayonnaise causes pale yellow stains. They are relatively easy to remove, but anything other than a tiny spot will spread readily.

Removal
Moderate

 Scrape off as much excess mayonnaise as possible with a spoon or blunt knife. Mix bicarbonate of soda with a little cold water to make a thick paste, apply to the stain and leave for 30 minutes or until it has dried completely, then brush off.

Alternatively, work a little washing-up liquid into both sides of the stain. Leave for 5 minutes before soaking in a bucket of water to which ½ cup washing-up liquid has been added. Leave to soak for 30 minutes.

Launder in the hottest water that is safe for the fabric in a 50/50 detergent/bicarbonate of soda wash.

On carpets and upholstery, scrape off and apply the paste as above to absorb excess mayonnaise. Leave for several hours – overnight if possible – then vacuum. If the stain persists, squirt a tiny amount of shaving cream over the stain and brush gently into the fibres with an old toothbrush. Wipe away excess foam with a clean dry cloth and blot with a sponge dipped in cold water.

 Scrape off excess mayonnaise as above, then spot treat with grease-solvent stain remover (see page 7). Rinse the solvent thoroughly from the fabric and air dry before laundering. If the stain persists, rub in biological (enzyme) liquid detergent. Leave this on and launder with biological (enzyme) detergent in the hottest water that is safe for the fabric.

MEDICINES Various

Staining from medicines will come from the syrups, which can be iron, alcohol or oil based.

Removal
Moderate

Syrup stains are sticky and spread readily.

DON'T use soap of any kind – soap will set alcohol-based medicine stains.

 For iron-based stains, squeeze lemon juice over the stain and cover with salt. Leave in the sun. Reapply if necessary – do not allow the lemon to dry out until the stain has disappeared. Rinse in lukewarm water, then launder in the hottest water that is safe for the fabric.

For alcohol-based stains, drench the stain with soda water, dabbing at it until it disappears. If you don't have any soda water, soak in cold water. If the stain persists, rub a little washing-up liquid into the back. Leave for 10 minutes and rinse. Repeat as necessary.

For oil-based stains, cover the stain with bicarbonate of soda or talcum powder and leave for 15 minutes before brushing off. Rub a little washing-up liquid into both sides. Add a squirt of washing-up liquid to a bowl of warm water, agitate to make it froth up and leave to soak for 30 minutes. Rinse.

On carpets and upholstery, spray or sponge with soda water to saturate. Keep blotting and reapplying. If it persists, apply a weak solution of washing-up liquid and water and blot. Repeat as necessary.

 For iron-based stains, treat with a rust remover.

For alcohol-based stains, rub a biological (enzyme) liquid detergent into both sides of the stain. Soak in cold water for 30 minutes, gently agitating the back of the fabric against itself from time to time. If the stain persists, rub stain stick on both sides and launder with biological (enzyme) detergent.

For oil-based stains, spot treat with grease-solvent stain remover (see page 7). Rinse thoroughly before laundering with biological (enzyme) detergent.

METAL POLISH Special

This pale yellowish stain can be identified by smell.

Removal
Moderate

 Sponge off the excess polish and spot treat with eucalyptus oil or turpentine (see page 7). Rinse thoroughly and air dry.

 On non-washable fabrics, spot treat with dry-cleaning solvent. Rinse thoroughly and air dry.

If the stain persists, soak in a biological (enzyme) pre-soak for 30 minutes or rub biological (enzyme) liquid detergent into both sides of the stain. Leave this on and launder with biological (enzyme) detergent in the hottest water that is safe for the fabric.

MILDEW Special

Mildew is a grey to black fungal growth that thrives in dark, warm, damp conditions. The original infection site will be black, spreading out into a grey fan. Mildew stains often appear on clothes that have not been stored properly. Mildew can often be identified by smell before it is visible.

Removal
Easy

 Brush off excess mildew outdoors and rub with bar soap; or, if the item is dry, dip half a lemon in salt and rub over the stain. Launder.

Alternatively, soak in sour milk – make this by adding 1 teaspoon white vinegar to 1 cup milk. Colour test and then saturate both sides of the stain. Leave to dry in the sun and then launder.

On leather, mix equal parts methylated spirits and water and wipe over the stained area with an absorbent white cloth.

On carpets and upholstery, dilute a teaspoon of TCP or other antiseptic in 1 cup water and sponge on. Squirt a tiny amount of shaving cream over the stain and brush gently into the fibres with an old toothbrush. Wipe away excess foam with a clean dry cloth and blot with a sponge dipped in cold water. You can also use the antiseptic solution above on mildewed books and papers, wiping a little over the stain with a soft white cloth.

 Brush off excess mildew outdoors. Apply biological (enzyme) liquid detergent to both sides of the stain. Leave this on and launder with biological (enzyme) detergent in the hottest water that is safe for the fabric.

If the stain persists, soak in all-fabric bleach solution for 15 minutes, rinse and launder. If the stain still remains, and the fabric can take it, soak in chlorine bleach solution for 15 minutes, rinse and launder.

MILK Special

Milk leaves white, creamy stains. Treat immediately – if allowed to dry, milk (and cream) stains give off a horrible smell.

Removal
Easy

DON'T use hot water, tumble dry or iron until the stain has been removed completely – heat sets milk stains.

 Spot treat the back of the stain with soda water or soak the fabric immediately in cold water. Gently agitate the back of the fabric against itself or hold the back of the stain under cold running water and let it run through for 5 minutes or until the stain disappears.

On carpets and upholstery, spray or sponge with soda water, saturating the area. Keep blotting and reapplying soda water until the stain has lifted. If the stain persists, squirt a tiny amount of shaving cream over it and brush gently into the fibres with an old toothbrush. Wipe away excess foam with a clean dry cloth and blot with a sponge dipped in cold water.

 Wet the stain with cold water and apply stain stick to both sides of the stain. Launder with biological (enzyme) detergent in warm water.

Alternatively, rub biological (enzyme) liquid detergent into both sides of the stain on dry fabric, or make a paste from biological (enzyme) detergent and warm water and rub on to both sides of wet fabric, then launder.

On non-washable fabrics, dab with lukewarm water and treat with dry-cleaning spot remover.

For old, stubborn stains, rub biological (enzyme) detergent into the stain as above and leave to soak in cool water for 4 hours, gently agitating the back of the fabric against itself from time to time.

MORTAR Industrial

After DIY and building work, mortar residue will often be left on walls, floors or any other household surface.

Removal
Easy

To avoid using brick-cleaning acids, hire a sandblaster and power tools from hire centres to clean stained surfaces.

The milder acid treatment is a concrete- and grout-cleaning product containing phosphoric acid. Don't attempt to put acid on large lumps of mortar as this won't work. Chisel off any protrusions and sand down with a wire brush, then apply the acid treatment exactly as directed.

Specialist brick-cleaning muratic acid is available from builder's merchants and hardware stores but should only be used as a last resort.

 DANGER Muratic acid is extremely hazardous. It will attack anything with which it comes into contact, causing permanent damage. If you are not experienced at building work, seek professional help.

If you do use muratic acid, follow the instructions carefully – some products must be diluted. Wear fully protective clothing, gloves, goggles and mask.

Don't let the acid come into contact with anything. Don't inhale.

Don't store – take the container back to the hardware store for proper disposal.

MOSS **Organic**

These green algae stains appear on exterior surfaces like roofs and boats, and damp interior places like bathroom surfaces and aquariums.

Removal
Easy with the right product, though some areas (such as swimming pool linings) are much more troublesome

 Dilute ½ cup white vinegar, ½ cup ammonia and a squirt of washing-up liquid in 4.5 litres (1 gallon) warm water. Scrub over the stained area and then rinse thoroughly.

 Mix 3 parts oxygen bleach to 1 part water and add a squirt of washing-up liquid. Scrub over the stained area and rinse thoroughly.

Specialist products are available from aquarium suppliers, boat suppliers and hardware stores. Rot mould and mildew stain removers from boat suppliers are safe to use on fibreglass, fabrics, canvas, plastic, carpets, wood and painted surfaces. Dilute in water as directed.

For really stubborn stains, use a strong toilet-bowl cleaner containing hydrochloric acid, available from hardware stores.

 DANGER Follow the safety instructions exactly, and rinse thoroughly.

MUCUS Protein

Pale yellow to pale green stains.

Removal
Easy

DON'T use hot water, tumble dry or iron until the stain has been removed completely – heat sets mucus stains.

 Wipe off as much excess mucus as possible with kitchen towels. Rinse immediately under cold running water or soak in cold water, gently agitating the back of the fabric against itself.

Bleach whites and baby clothes with lemon juice and leave in the sun to dry.

On carpets and upholstery, wipe off excess mucus as above, then spray or sponge with soda water, saturating the area. Keep blotting and reapplying soda water until the stain has lifted. If the stain persists, squirt a tiny amount of shaving cream over the stain and brush gently into the fibres with an old toothbrush. Wipe away excess foam with a clean dry cloth and blot with a sponge dipped in warm water.

On non-washable fabrics, dilute 1 teaspoon ammonia in lukewarm water and sponge over the stain. If it persists, dry clean as soon as possible.

 Gently agitate the back of the fabric against itself in cold water with biological (enzyme) detergent or pre-soak, then leave to soak overnight. If the stain persists, cover both sides with biological (enzyme) liquid detergent or stain stick and launder in warm water.

On carpets and upholstery, clean up the excess as above. Make a solution from water, biological (enzyme) detergent and a little disinfectant and sponge over the stain. Treat any remaining stain with soda water.

MUD Protein

These stains are usually brown. Red mud should be treated as for rust stains (see page 104).

Removal
Easy

DON'T use hot water, tumble dry or iron until the stain has been completely removed.

 Always allow mud stains to dry out completely before tackling them. When dried, shake out and brush off as much excess as possible with a stiff brush or vacuum.

For light stains, cut a potato in half, rub it over the stain and launder.

For heavy stains, once the mud has dried, mix equal parts cold water and methylated spirits and sponge on. If the fabric is colourfast, use neat white vinegar.

For fresh stains on carpets and upholstery, sprinkle with bicarbonate of soda, talcum powder or salt and leave to dry, then vacuum. Repeat as necessary. When you have lifted all you can, squirt a tiny amount of shaving cream over the stain and brush gently into the fibres with an old toothbrush. Wipe away excess foam with a clean dry cloth and blot with a sponge dipped in cold water.

 Dry and brush off excess mud as before. Rub biological (enzyme) liquid detergent into the back and leave to soak in cool water for 30 minutes, then launder with biological (enzyme) detergent.

Alternatively, soak in biological (enzyme) pre-soak and launder as above.

On non-washable fabrics, dilute biological (enzyme) liquid detergent in water and spot treat the stain (see page 7). If the stain persists, take to the dry cleaner as soon as possible.

MUSTARD Dye

Mustard is an oily mixture that contains yellow dye pigment.

Removal
Difficult

DON'T use hot water, tumble dry or iron, and don't use ammonia – both heat and ammonia will set mustard stains.

 Scrape off as much excess mustard as possible with a spoon or blunt knife, then rub glycerine over the back of the stain and leave for 1 hour.

Squirt a little washing-up liquid into ½ cup warm water and add 1 tablespoon white vinegar. Colour test and then spot treat, blotting at the back of the stain (see page 7). Rinse thoroughly before laundering.

 Apply biological (enzyme) liquid detergent to the back of the stain and scrub with an old toothbrush or nailbrush. Launder with biological (enzyme) detergent in the hottest water that is safe for the fabric.

If the stain persists, soak in all-fabric bleach solution for 15 minutes, rinse and launder. If the stain still remains, and the fabric can take it, soak in chlorine bleach solution for 15 minutes, rinse and launder.

On carpets and upholstery, scrape off excess mustard as above, then sponge with soda water or cold water and scrub with carpet shampoo. If the stain has dried in, mix equal parts glycerine and water and apply first to loosen the fibres.

Take non-washable fabrics to the dry cleaner as soon as possible.

NAIL VARNISH Lacquer

This fast-drying lacquer polish can be any colour or clear.

Removal
Moderate

 Blot up as much excess nail varnish as possible with an absorbent white cloth, working from the outside of the stain inwards to avoid spreading it any further, then spot treat with methylated spirits (see page 7). Rinse and launder.

For irreversible carpet spots, bleach with a few drops of lemon juice or white vinegar. To re-dye, rub a slightly dampened spare piece of carpet over the stain, or fill in with felt-tip pen or ink.

 Blot up excess nail varnish as above, then spot treat with white spirit, amyl acetate or a non-oily nail varnish remover, blotting at the back of the stain. Rinse the solvent thoroughly from the fabric and air dry before laundering with biological (enzyme) detergent.

On carpets and upholstery, blot up excess as above. Colour test and then blot, alternating between amyl acetate or non-oily nail varnish remover and cool water. Scrub with carpet or upholstery shampoo.

For irreversible carpet spots, bleach with a few drops of 3 per cent hydrogen peroxide bleach (NOT hair bleach, see page 16) and re-colour as above.

Take non-washable fabrics to the dry cleaner as soon as possible.

NEWSPRINT Combination

Newspapers can leave black, smudgy stains.

Removal
Moderate

 Spot treat with methylated spirits (see page 7), rinse and launder. This method works on both washable and non-washable fabrics.

If the stain persists, add 4 tablespoons ammonia to 1 litre (2 pints) warm water and colour test. Leave to soak for several hours or overnight, then rinse thoroughly. To neutralize all traces of the ammonia, mix a solution of equal parts white vinegar and water and spot treat or soak for 1 hour.

 Apply biological (enzyme) liquid detergent to the front. Leave this on and launder with biological (enzyme) detergent in the hottest water that is safe for the fabric.

If the stain persists, soak for 15 minutes in all-fabric bleach solution and rinse thoroughly. If the stain still remains, and the fabric can take it, soak for 15 minutes in chlorine bleach solution.

OIL **Greasy**

Oil stains quickly penetrate the fibres of fabrics and carpets, and are liable to spread if not treated carefully. The stain is likely to be deeper in colour at the centre, fading to a paler shade towards the edges.

Removal
Moderate

 Dab up as much excess oil as possible with kitchen towels or an absorbent white cloth, then sprinkle with bicarbonate of soda, cornflour or talcum powder and rub gently into the stain. Leave for 30 minutes to allow the powder to absorb the oil, then wipe off with a dry flannel facecloth. This method works on both washable and non-washable fabrics.

Alternatively, work a little washing-up liquid into both sides. Leave for 5 minutes before soaking in a bucket of water to which ½ cup washing-up liquid has been added. Leave for 30 minutes.

Launder in the hottest water that is safe for the fabric in a 50/50 detergent/bicarbonate of soda wash.

On carpets and upholstery, dab up and sprinkle with powder as above. Leave for several hours – overnight if possible – then vacuum. If the stain persists, squirt a tiny amount of shaving cream over the stain and brush gently into the fibres with an old toothbrush. Wipe away excess foam with a clean dry cloth and blot with a sponge dipped in cold water.

 Dab up and sprinkle with powder as above to absorb excess oil, then spot treat with a grease-solvent stain remover (see page 7). Rinse thoroughly from the fabric and air dry before laundering. If the stain persists, rub in biological (enzyme) liquid detergent. Leave this on and launder with biological (enzyme) detergent in the hottest water that is safe for the fabric.

OINTMENT Greasy

Designed to penetrate and protect the skin, ointment stains are thick and greasy-looking, and come in varying colours from yellow to purple. They can be identified by a strong smell.

Removal
Moderate

 Scrape off as much excess ointment as possible with a spoon or old credit card, working from the outside of the stain inwards to avoid spreading it further, then sprinkle with bicarbonate of soda, cornflour or talcum powder and rub gently into the stain. Leave for 30 minutes to allow the powder to absorb the ointment, then wipe off with a dry flannel facecloth. This method works on both washable and non-washable fabrics.

Alternatively, work a little washing-up liquid into both sides. Leave for 5 minutes before soaking in a bucket of water to which ½ cup washing-up liquid has been added. Leave for 30 minutes.

Launder in the hottest water that is safe for the fabric in a 50/50 detergent/bicarbonate of soda wash.

On carpets and upholstery, scrape up and sprinkle with powder as above to absorb excess ointment. Leave for several hours – overnight if possible – then vacuum. If the stain persists, squirt a tiny amount of shaving cream over the stain and brush gently into the fibres with an old toothbrush. Wipe away excess foam with a clean dry cloth and blot with a sponge dipped in cold water.

 Scrape off excess ointment as above, then spot treat with grease-solvent stain remover (see page 7). Rinse thoroughly and air dry, then launder with biological (enzyme) detergent in the hottest water that is safe for the fabric.

Treat stubborn stains on carpets with dry-cleaning solvent. Apply carefully, avoiding the carpet backing, then sponge off with a clean, damp cloth.

PAINT, LATEX Tannin

Water based with a small element of solvent, latex paint is more durable and tougher than oil-based paint and less likely to fade or attract mildew. It is widely used on exteriors like boats and buildings.

Removal
Easy while still wet; difficult when dried

 Blot up as much excess paint as possible with kitchen towels. Mix 1 teaspoon non-bleach liquid detergent in 1 cup lukewarm water. Dip the stain in the water and gently agitate the back of the fabric against itself.
Spot treat dried-in stains with methylated spirits (see page 7). Rinse and launder.

 Blot up excess paint as above, then spot treat with nail varnish remover. Spot treat stubborn stains with grease-solvent stain remover. Rinse thoroughly from the fabric and air dry, then launder. If the stain persists, rub biological (enzyme) liquid detergent into both sides and launder with biological (enzyme) detergent in the hottest water that is safe for the fabric.

PAINT, OIL Greasy

These thick, rich stains can be any colour and are identified by the smell.

Removal
Difficult – often impossible if dried in

 Spot treat with turpentine, dabbing gently at the back of the fabric (see page 7). Rinse and launder.

 Spot treat with white spirit or solvent paint remover. Rinse thoroughly from the fabric and air dry, then launder. If the stain persists, rub in biological (enzyme) liquid detergent, then launder with biological (enzyme) detergent in the hottest water that is safe for the fabric.

PAINT, TEMPERA Tannin

Paint used to paint classrooms.

Removal
Moderate

Tempera paint is made with pigments chosen to fade in strong light, so any residue left after stain removal may disappear when left to dry in the sun.

 If the paint spill is still wet, hold the back of the fabric under a running cold tap, gently agitating the back of the fabric against itself. Then wash with soap in lukewarm water.
If the paint has dried, scrape off the dried surface and treat as above.

 Treat stubborn stains with a stain stick.

PAINT, WATER BASED Tannin

Water-based paint is supplied in all sizes from artist's palettes to large cans of household emulsion. It spreads very easily.

Removal
Easy while still wet; moderate when dried

 Scrape off as much excess paint as possible with a spoon or old credit card and rinse immediately in cold water while still wet, gently agitating the back of the fabric against itself. If the paint has dried in, rub the stain with bar soap first.

Spot treat with ammonia, dabbing at the back of the stain (see page 7). Colour test first – if the fabric is non-colourfast, dilute 1 part ammonia to 4 parts water. To neutralize all traces of the ammonia, mix a solution of equal parts white vinegar and water and spot treat or soak for 1 hour.

Sponge non-washable fabrics with cold water. If the stain persists, dry clean as soon as possible.

On carpets and upholstery, sponge with cold water. Cover large spills with lots of cold water, then put plenty of towels or kitchen towels over the stain and leave to soak up the excess paint. If the stain persists, dab with ammonia (colour test first) or methylated spirits.

 Scrape off excess paint as above, then spot treat with tannin stain remover. If the stain persists, rub in biological (enzyme) liquid detergent. Leave this on and launder with biological (enzyme) detergent in the hottest water that is safe for the fabric.

PEANUT BUTTER Tannin

Peanut butter leaves yellowish, nutty-smelling stains.

Removal
Easy

DON'T use any kind of soap – soap sets peanut butter stains.

 Scrape off as much excess peanut butter as possible with a spoon or old credit card, working from the outside of the stain inwards to avoid spreading it any further. Rinse in cold water.

Rub liquid detergent into both sides and leave for 5 minutes. Stretch the fabric right side down over a sink, bowl or saucepan, securing with clothes pegs or an elastic band. Pour through the hottest water that is safe for the fabric from the back of the stain, from as high as possible without danger of splashing.

For old, stubborn stains, mix equal parts white vinegar and warm water. Colour test, then sponge on to the stain and leave to dry in the sun. Repeat as necessary. Alternatively, rub the back of the stain with glycerine, leave for 1 hour and rinse.

On non-washable fabrics, scrape off excess peanut butter as before, dab with cold water and apply a little washing-up liquid. Dab with cool water, working from the outside of the stain inwards to avoid spreading it any further. Alternatively, sprinkle with borax, rub in gently and leave for 5 minutes, then dab with cool water. If this doesn't work, take to the dry cleaner as soon as possible.

On carpets and upholstery, scrape off excess peanut butter as before, then squirt over a tiny amount of shaving cream and brush gently into the fibres with an old toothbrush. Wipe away excess foam with a clean dry cloth and blot with a sponge dipped in cold water.

 Scrape off excess as before, then apply stain stick to both sides and launder with biological (enzyme) detergent in the hottest water that is safe for the fabric.

For old, stubborn stains, mix 1 part 3 per cent hydrogen peroxide bleach (NOT hair bleach, see page 16) with 6 parts water and colour test. Soak for 15 minutes, then rinse and launder as usual.

PENCIL MARKS Special

Pencil leaves grey graphite marks, often in long thin lines.

Removal
Moderate

 First, try a pencil eraser. Use the smallest, lightest strokes so as not to spread the stain any further.

If this doesn't work, gently rub liquid detergent on to both sides of the stain and rinse in warm water.

If the stain persists, add 4 tablespoons ammonia to 1 litre (2 pints) warm water and colour test. Leave to soak for several hours or overnight, then rinse thoroughly. To neutralize all traces of the ammonia, mix a solution of equal parts white vinegar and water and spot treat or soak for 1 hour (see page 7).

On non-washable fabrics, colour test, then apply ammonia to the back and dab off. Repeat as necessary. If this doesn't work, dry clean as soon as possible.

 Spot treat with a specialist pencil-mark stain remover. Rinse thoroughly, then launder with biological (enzyme) detergent in the hottest water that is safe for the fabric.

PERFUME Tannin

A combination of natural and chemical oils, perfumes leave light, strong-smelling stains.

Removal
Easy

DON'T use any kind of soap – soap sets perfume stains.

 Using kitchen towels or an absorbent white cloth, gently blot the back of the stain with soda water. If you don't have any, use cold water.

If the stain persists, work a little washing-up liquid into both sides of the stain. Leave for 10 minutes, then rinse in cool water, gently agitating the back of fabric against itself.

If the stain still remains, dilute 1 tablespoon white vinegar in 1 litre (2 pints) warm water and add a squirt of washing-up liquid. Colour test, then agitate to froth it up and leave to soak for 15 minutes, then rinse.

 Cover both sides with biological (enzyme) liquid detergent, or with a paste made from powdered biological (enzyme) detergent and cool water. Leave this on and launder with biological (enzyme) detergent in the hottest water that is safe for the fabric.

Alternatively, wet the stain with cold water and apply stain stick to both sides of the fabric. Launder in the hottest water that is safe for the fabric.

PERSPIRATION Tannin

Fresh stains are barely visible and are normally acidic. Older stains turn alkaline and yellow.

Removal
Easy if wet; moderate if dried in

Drying at low temperatures stops perspiration stains turning yellow.

DON'T use any kind of soap – soap sets perspiration stains.

 For fresh stains, dilute 1 tablespoon white vinegar in 250 ml (½ pint) water. Colour test, then sponge on, leave for 15 minutes and rinse. Repeat as necessary.

Alternatively, wet the fabric and rub bar soap over the stain. Work into a lather and leave out in the sun. Keep moist, spraying with warm water every 15 minutes or so. Don't let it dry out. When the marks have risen to the surface of the fabric, rinse thoroughly.

Spot treat dried-in stains with ammonia (see page 7). Colour test – if the fabric is non-fast, dilute 1 part ammonia with 4 parts water. To neutralize all traces of ammonia, mix a solution of equal parts white vinegar and water and spot treat or soak for 1 hour. Air dry in the sun if possible – sunlight is a natural bleach.

To get rid of perspiration odour, dilute 2 tablespoons salt in a bowl of warm water. Soak for 1 hour, rinse and launder.

On non-washable fabrics, add 1 tablespoon cream of tartar and 3 crushed aspirins to a little warm water to make a paste. Apply to the stain and leave for 30 minutes. Dab off with lukewarm water.

 Soak fresh stains in a biological (enzyme) pre-soak for 30 minutes. Launder with biological (enzyme) detergent in the hottest water that is safe for the fabric.

If the stain persists, soak in all-fabric bleach solution for 15 minutes, rinse and launder. If the stain still remains, and the fabric can take it, soak in chlorine bleach solution for 15 minutes, rinse and launder.

PET HAIR **Special**

Pets that live outside will usually only shed hair once or twice a year. House pets are likely to shed hair all year round because they are not exposed to seasonal temperature changes. Regular grooming reduces the problem.

Removal
Easy

 Brush with a special pet hair mitt made from hooked fibres. Alternatively, use a pet hair removing sponge or sponge paintbrush.

You can also buy a special roller with adhesive tape that will lift the hairs as it rolls over them. For small areas, like laps and chairs, you can use ordinary adhesive tape or wider industrial tape to lift the hairs. Cut off lengths and apply the sticky side to the surface, lifting and replacing as the tape fills with hairs.

 Treat with a pet hair removal product, available from specialist suppliers.

PET URINE Protein

These are often first identified by smell. A black light bulb will reveal all urine stains, even old ones. Turn out the lights and shine it over all areas accessible to your pet: if there are old stains that are visible only with the bulb, draw a light chalk mark around each one. It is crucial to remove all the smells so that the pet isn't tempted to return to that spot. If possible, make the area impossible for it to get to.

Removal
Easy to moderate

DON'T use hot water or steam cleaners – heat will set the odour.

DON'T use any strong-smelling chemicals, especially white vinegar and ammonia – they might make the area more attractive to your pet.

 Launder, adding ½ cup bicarbonate of soda to the detergent tray. Don't tumble dry with any heat – air dry or cool tumble dry.

On carpets and upholstery, blot up as much excess urine as possible with kitchen towels and newspaper. Spray or sponge with soda water, saturating the area. Keep blotting and reapplying until the stain has lifted.

If it is an old stain or a place your pet returns to repeatedly, you might have to go a stage further in saturating the area to get rid of any chemical residue that will react with the proteins in the urine – which is what makes your pet return to the same spot. Buy, rent or borrow a wet-vac, which will force clean water through the fabric or carpet.

 On carpets and upholstery, blot up excess urine with soda water as above and then use a pet odour neutralizer, available from specialist suppliers. Shampoo with pet stain-removal carpet shampoo.

Wash down walls and skirting boards with a biological (enzyme) detergent diluted in warm water. The acid in urine stains may permanently discolour varnish on wooden floors or paint on skirting boards: the only treatment is to remove and replace.

PETROL Greasy

Petrol leaves pale brown and greasy stains.

Removal
Moderate

Petrol stains left longer than 24 hours on polyester, nylon or nylon/polyester blends will be very difficult to remove.

 Dab up as much excess petrol as possible with kitchen towels or an absorbent white cloth, then sprinkle with bicarbonate of soda, cornflour or talcum powder and rub gently into the stain. Leave for 30 minutes to allow the powder to absorb the oil, then wipe off with a dry flannel facecloth. This method works on both washable and non-washable fabrics.

Alternatively, work a little washing-up liquid into both sides of the stain. Leave for 5 minutes, before soaking in a bucket of water to which ½ cup washing-up liquid has been added. Leave to soak for at least 30 minutes.

If the stain persists, mix bicarbonate of soda with a little cold water to make a thick paste and apply. Leave for 30 minutes or until it has dried in completely, then brush off.

Launder in the hottest water that is safe for the fabric in a 50/50 detergent/bicarbonate of soda wash.

On carpets and upholstery, dab and sprinkle with powder as before to absorb excess petrol. Leave for several hours – overnight if possible – then vacuum. Dilute 1 tablespoon borax in 500 ml (1 pint) warm water and sponge on to the stain, alternating with clean warm water as the stain is removed. If the stain persists, squirt on a tiny amount of shaving cream and brush gently into the fibres with an old toothbrush. Wipe away excess foam with a clean dry cloth and blot with a sponge dipped in cold water.

Dab and sprinkle with powder as before to absorb excess petrol, then rub biological (enzyme) detergent into both sides of the stain on dry fabric. Leave this on and launder with biological (enzyme) detergent in the hottest water that is safe for the fabric.

If the stain persists, soak in all-fabric bleach solution for 15 minutes, rinse and launder. If the stain still remains, and the fabric can take it, soak in chlorine bleach solution for 15 minutes, rinse and launder.

DANGER Extreme caution must be taken when dealing with petrol stains, as they make clothing more inflammable than normal.

DANGER Don't use solvent-based stain removers, as petrol is highly inflammable.

DANGER Don't put in the tumble dryer, even after rinsing – always air dry.

PICKLE/CHUTNEY/RELISH **Combination**

These oily/waxy brown or yellow stains also contain dye and can be identified by smell.

Removal
Moderate – easy if still wet

 Rinse as soon as possible under cold running water, gently agitating the back of the fabric against itself and letting the water run through. Colour test and then dab white vinegar all over the back of the stain and rinse through again. Repeat several times.

Rub liquid detergent into the back of the stain and launder in the hottest water that is safe for the fabric.

Alternatively, rub glycerine into the back of the stain and leave to soak in warm, soapy water for 1 hour.

 Rinse as soon as possible under cold water as above.

Spot treat with red-wine stain remover (see page 7), then rinse the solvent thoroughly from the fabric and air dry before laundering. If traces of the stain remain, rub biological (enzyme) liquid detergent into both sides of the stain. Leave this on and launder with biological (enzyme) detergent in the hottest water that is safe for the fabric.

If the stain persists, soak in all-fabric bleach solution for 15 minutes, rinse and launder. If the stain remains, and the fabric can take it, soak in chlorine bleach solution for 15 minutes, rinse and launder.

PLANT STAINS **Combination**

Leaf stains leave a brown residue. Pollen stains are a fine, powdery yellow, often with some dust residue still on the surface.

Removal
Easy to difficult

Stains from leaves and tree pollen will usually rinse out. Flower pollen stains can be very difficult to remove – they cling to the fabric with tiny hooked burrs that fold over on to the fibres once they have got a grip.

 For light leaf stains, cut a potato in half, rub it over the stain and launder.

For flower pollen stains, shake out the fabric to get rid of any excess powder. If the stain is on a garment or other portable fabric, leaving it lying in the sun for a day is sometimes enough to get rid of the stain.

Alternatively, vacuuming can dislodge the hook-like grip the burrs have on fabric or carpet. Then try laying a strip of adhesive tape gently on to the stain and pulling it away from the fabric to remove the pollen.

If the stain persists, soak in cool water, gently agitating the back of the fabric against itself.

For really tough pollen stains, spot treat with a solution of equal parts cold water and methylated spirits (see page 7). If colourfast, use white vinegar.

For fresh leaf or pollen stains on carpets and upholstery, squirt on a little shaving foam and brush with an old toothbrush. Wipe away excess foam with a clean dry cloth and rinse.

 Spot treat with dry-cleaning solvent and air dry. Rub a little biological (enzyme) liquid detergent into the stain, then launder with biological (enzyme) detergent in the hottest water that is safe for the fabric.

Bleaching may be the only solution for pollen stains on fabrics. Soak in all-fabric bleach solution for 15 minutes, rinse and launder. If the stain remains, and the fabric can take it, soak in chlorine bleach solution for 15 minutes, rinse and launder.

Use a carpet stain remover on carpets and upholstery.

PLASTIC MODELLING CLAY Greasy

Plastic modelling clay leaves a greasy, waxy residue in various colours.

Removal
Moderate

 Scrape off as much excess modelling clay as possible with an old spoon or blunt knife. Sprinkle borax on to the back of the stain and rub in gently, then hold the back of the stain under cool running water.

Alternatively, mix bicarbonate of soda with a little cold water to make a thick paste, apply to the stain and leave for 30 minutes or until it has dried completely, then brush off.

Launder in the hottest water that is safe for the fabric in a 50/50 detergent/bicarbonate of soda wash.

 Scrape off excess modelling clay as above. Spot treat with a grease-solvent stain remover. Rinse thoroughly from the fabric and air dry before laundering. If the stain persists, rub biological (enzyme) liquid detergent into both sides of the stain. Leave this on and launder with biological (enzyme) detergent in the hottest water that is safe for the fabric.

If modelling clay has been squashed into carpets or upholstery, stiffen with a bag of ice and scrape off as much as you can with a spoon or blunt knife. Apply a grease stain-removal carpet or upholstery shampoo.

PLAY PUTTY Greasy

Modelling clay leaves a greasy/waxy residue in various primary colours.

Removal
Moderate

 Put in the freezer to harden off the putty, then pick off as much excess as possible with your fingernails or a blunt knife. Sprinkle borax on to the back and rub in gently, then hold the back of the stain under cool running water. If you do not have borax, use salt.

Alternatively, mix bicarbonate of soda with a little cold water to make a thick paste, apply and leave until it has dried completely, then brush off.

Launder in the hottest water that is safe for the fabric in a 50/50 detergent/bicarbonate of soda wash.

Spot treat stubborn stains with methylated spirits (see page 7). Rinse and launder.

 Freeze and scrape off excess putty as above. Spot treat grease-solvent stain remover, dabbing at the back of the stain. Rinse thoroughly from the fabric and air dry, then launder. If the stain persists, rub biological (enzyme) liquid detergent into both sides of the stain. Leave this on and launder with biological (enzyme) detergent in the hottest water that is safe for the fabric.

If play putty has been squashed into carpets or upholstery, pick off as much as you can, then apply a grease stain-removal carpet or upholstery shampoo.

RESIN Organic

Resin is a watery, sticky sap containing sugar, salt and minerals that in the home issues from Christmas trees, pine cones and any soft wooden surface warmed by sunlight or other heat.

Removal
Moderate

 Scrape off as much excess resin as possible with a spoon or blunt knife, then spot treat with glycerine, tapping at the back of the stain with an old toothbrush or spoon (see page 7). If it has dried in, warm the glycerine a little before applying. Rub washing-up liquid into the back and rinse under cool running water, gently agitating the back of the fabric against itself.

If the stain persists, spot treat with turpentine.

 Apply resin or sap stain remover to both sides of the stain and leave for 10 minutes or as directed. If the stain persists, rub biological (enzyme) liquid detergent into both sides and launder with biological (enzyme) detergent in the hottest water that is safe for the fabric.

For old, tough stains, spot treat with dry-cleaning solvent. Rinse thoroughly from the fabric and air dry before laundering with biological (enzyme) detergent.

If any colour still remains, treat as a dye stain (see page 57).

Dry clean non-washable fabrics as soon as possible.

ROUGE Combination

This cosmetic leaves a greasy or powdery red stain.

Removal
Moderate

Rouge spreads readily, so always work from the outside of the stain inwards.

 Moisten the stain and apply bar soap, washing-up liquid or liquid detergent to both sides. Gently agitate the back of the fabric against itself in warm water, and rinse thoroughly. Repeat as necessary.

Alternatively, soak in warm detergent for 30 minutes.

 Moisten the stain and apply stain stick to both sides. Launder with biological (enzyme) detergent in the hottest water that is safe for the fabric.

RUBBER MARKS Special

Rubber heels and soles, and skid marks from tricycle and bike wheels, can leave nasty black marks on floors, stone being especially vulnerable. Always test any stain-removal procedure on a hidden area of the floor first.

Removal
Moderate

Marks left untreated any longer than a week will be very difficult to remove.

DON'T use a water-based cleaner, or a cleaner that has to be rinsed off, on wood floors.

 Try rubbing out the marks with a pencil eraser.

On waxed floors, rub turpentine on to the mark. This will remove any wax coating along with the stain and the area will have to be re-waxed.

 Anything but a very fine scouring powder may leave scratch marks. If you do use it, rub very lightly.

On non-waxed floors, use a specialist solvent-based cleaning product. Apply directly to the stain and dab at the mark with a non-abrasive nylon pad. Rinse well.

Alternatively, rub with very fine steel wool and floor detergent. Wipe dry and apply polish immediately.

Stubborn old marks can be removed manually with a buffer-pad tool attachment. Consult a professional.

On stone floors, mix equal parts white spirit and warm water with a squirt of washing-up liquid. Rub on gently, working from the outside inwards with your fingertip inside a cloth or using a cotton bud. Rinse.

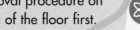

103

RUST **Organic**

These reddish brown marks can appear anywhere, from carpets after old radiators have been taken out to old cooking saucepans and tins, neglected toilet bowls or on clothing.

Removal
Moderate

DON'T use chlorine bleach – it sets rust stains.

 On carpets and upholstery, mix equal parts ammonia and boiling water and leave to cool. Colour test, then sponge on to the rust and rinse off.

On cooking pans, dip half a potato in salt or bicarbonate of soda and rub over the rust.

On clothing, cover the marks with lemon juice and leave to dry in the sun.

Alternatively, cover rust spots with cream of tartar and soak in hot water for 15 minutes, then launder.

On toilet bowls, sprinkle citric acid all over the rust and leave for 1 hour. Scrub with a toilet brush and flush. Or sprinkle with borax and leave overnight.

A damp pumice stone will remove rust from most surfaces, but don't use on metal or aluminium.

 On metals, fabrics, carpets and upholstery, treat with a rust remover.

 DANGER Rust removers are highly poisonous liquid solvents containing hydrofluoric acid and oxalic acid. Handle with care. Follow all safety instructions exactly.

Patio, drive and paving cleaner works well on rust stains in toilet bowls.

On concrete floors, dissolve 500 g (1 lb) oxalic acid powder (sold as wood bleach at builder's merchants and hardware stores) in 4.5 litres (1 gallon) water. Soak for 3 hours. Rinse and scrub with a stiff broom.

 DANGER Handle with extreme caution (see above).

SALAD DRESSING, CREAMY **Greasy**

A mixture of egg yolks, oils and lemon juice, salad dressing causes pale yellow stains. These are relatively easy to remove, but anything other than a tiny spot will spread readily.

 Scrape off as much excess dressing as possible with a spoon or blunt knife. Mix bicarbonate of soda with a little cold water to make a thick paste, apply and leave until it has dried completely, then brush off.

Alternatively, work a little washing-up liquid into both sides. Leave for 5 minutes before soaking in a bucket of water to which ½ cup washing-up liquid

Removal
Moderate

has been added. Leave for 30 minutes. Launder in the hottest water that is safe for the fabric in a 50/50 detergent/bicarbonate of soda wash.

On carpets and upholstery, scrape off excess dressing and apply the paste as before. Leave for several hours – overnight if possible – then vacuum. If the stain persists, squirt a tiny amount of shaving cream over the stain and brush gently into the fibres with an old toothbrush. Wipe away excess foam with a clean dry cloth and blot with a sponge dipped in cold water.

 Scrape off excess dressing as before, then spot treat with grease-solvent stain remover (see page 7). Rinse thoroughly from the fabric and air dry, then launder. If the stain persists, rub in biological (enzyme) liquid detergent and launder with biological (enzyme) detergent in the hottest water that is safe for the fabric.

SALAD DRESSING, VINAIGRETTE **Combination**

Vinaigrette salad dressing consists of a combination of oil, vinegar and herbs which leaves a brownish, greasy stain that may be flecked with spots of pepper or herbs.

Removal
Difficult – these stains combine very readily with oxygen in the air and, once oxidized, can be impossible to remove

 Work a little washing-up liquid into both sides of the stain. Leave for 5 minutes before soaking in a bucket of water to which ½ cup washing-up liquid has been added. Leave for 30 minutes.

If the stain persists, mix bicarbonate of soda with a little cold water to make a thick paste, apply and leave until it has dried completely, then brush off. Launder in the hottest water that is safe for the fabric in a 50/50 detergent/bicarbonate of soda wash.

On carpets and upholstery, mop up as much vinaigrette as possible with kitchen towels. Work a little undiluted washing-up liquid into the stain and sponge off with hot water. Repeat as necessary.

 Spot treat with grease-solvent stain remover (see page 7). Rinse the solvent thoroughly from the fabric and air dry before laundering.

If the stain persists, rub in biological (enzyme) liquid detergent and launder with biological (enzyme) detergent in the hottest water that is safe for the fabric.

Dry clean non-washable fabrics as soon as possible.

SAUCE Combination

Sauce of various kinds leaves a brown, cream or red stain.

Removal
Moderate

 Rinse as soon as possible under cold running water, holding the back of the stain under the tap and letting the water run through. Colour test. Dab white vinegar all over the back and rinse through again. Repeat.

Work liquid detergent into the back of the stain and launder in the hottest water that is safe for the fabric.

Alternatively, rub glycerine into the back, then launder in the hottest water that is safe for the fabric.

 Rinse as soon as possible under cold water as above.

Spot treat with red-wine stain remover, dabbing at the back of the stain (see page 7). Rinse thoroughly from the fabric and then air dry before laundering.

If traces of the stain remain, rub biological (enzyme) liquid detergent into both sides of the stain. Leave this on and launder with biological (enzyme) detergent in the hottest water that is safe for the fabric.

If the stain persists, soak in all-fabric bleach solution for 15 minutes, rinse and launder. If the stain still remains, and the fabric can take it, soak in chlorine bleach solution for 15 minutes, rinse and launder.

SCORCH Special

These grey or black marks are caused by slight burning from ironing, cigarette burns, cooking burns and so on.

Removal
Difficult – severe marks cannot be removed

DON'T use any kind of soap – soap sets scorch marks.

 Rinse under the full force of a running cold tap, then dilute 1 tablespoon borax in 1 litre (2 pints) warm water and soak for 1 hour. Launder in the hottest water that is safe for the fabric. Brush any remaining traces with an emery board.

For small marks on woollens, rub the mark with the edge of a silver coin.

For small marks on carpets, snip off the scorched ends of the fibres with a sharp pair of scissors, then rub with the side of a silver coin. On fine tufted carpets and upholstery, gently rub fine wire wool in circular movements over the mark.

 Colour test, then sponge with a cold solution of 1 part 3 per cent hydrogen peroxide bleach (NOT hair bleach, see page 16) to 4 parts water. Cover with a clean white absorbent cloth and press a warm iron over the cloth – don't allow it to come into direct contact with the fabric. Repeat the sponging and ironing until you have removed as much of the mark as possible. Spray on a spot stain remover and launder.

If the mark persists, soak in all-fabric bleach solution for 15 minutes, rinse and launder. If the mark still remains, and the fabric can take it, soak in chlorine bleach solution for 15 minutes, rinse and launder.

Don't attempt to remove scorch marks from non-washable fabrics; dry clean as soon as possible.

Anything other than small marks on carpets and upholstery will require professional treatment.

SEALANTS Industrial

Deep-penetrating sealants are used as invisible protective barriers against all kinds of grease, dirt and stains on tiles, floorings and so on. The stains are usually grey, but can come in many different shades to match bathroom interiors.

Removal

Difficult – any spills should be removed immediately with clean rags or soap and water before they have time to set

 If the stain has dried into clothing, freeze for 30 minutes. Scrape and pick off as much sealant as possible with your fingernails and a blunt knife.

Work liquid detergent into both sides of the stain, leave for 15 minutes and rinse.

 Freeze and scrape as above, then soak in all-fabric or chlorine bleach solution, as safe for the fabric, for 15 minutes. Rinse and launder.

Alternatively, spot treat with solvent stain remover (see page 7). Rinse the solvent thoroughly from the fabric and air dry before laundering. If the stain persists, rub in biological (enzyme) liquid detergent. Leave this on and launder with biological (enzyme) detergent in the hottest water that is safe for the fabric.

On carpets, blot up as much sealant as possible with kitchen towels. Wearing gloves and a face mask, dab the stain with isopropyl alcohol using an absorbent white cloth. Don't apply this directly to the stain, as it may sink through the carpet and damage the foam backing. Rinse, then apply a weak washing-up liquid solution and blot alternately with a wet cloth and a dry cloth, soaking up the remaining residue.

If the stain persists, colour test and then mix 1 part 3 per cent hydrogen peroxide bleach (NOT hair bleach, see page 16) with 2 parts water. Dab alternately with wet and dry cloths.

SEMEN **Protein**

Semen leaves white stains on sheets and underwear.

Removal
Easy

DON'T use hot water, tumble dry or iron until the stain has been removed completely – heat sets semen stains.

Rinse under cool running water, gently agitating the back of the fabric against itself.

Soak in a cool biological (enzyme) pre-soak for 30 minutes, or rub biological (enzyme) detergent into both sides of the stain and soak in cool water for 30 minutes, gently agitating the back of the fabric against itself from time to time.

SHOE WHITENER/CLEANER **Tannin**

These products produce fast-spreading, thick white, blue or red stains. Heavy stains will have a crust concealing liquid within.

Removal
Moderate

DON'T use any kind of soap – soap sets these stains.

Scrape off as much excess cleaner as possible with a spoon or blunt knife, working from the outside of the stain inwards to avoid spreading it further.

Rub liquid detergent, or a paste made from detergent and water, into the back. Scrub with a toothbrush dipped in the hottest water that is safe for the fabric.

If it persists, colour test, then spot treat with rubbing alcohol, dabbing at the back (see page 7). Rinse thoroughly from the fabric and air dry, then launder.

Scrape off excess cleaner as above, then spot treat with a tannin solvent or stain stick. Rinse thoroughly and air dry. If the stain persists, rub biological (enzyme) liquid detergent into both sides of the stain. Leave this on and launder with biological (enzyme) detergent in the hottest water that is safe for the fabric.

If the stain persists, soak in all-fabric bleach solution for 15 minutes, rinse and launder. If the stain still remains, and the fabric can take it, soak in chlorine bleach solution for 15 minutes, rinse and launder.

On non-washable fabrics, carefully scrape off excess cleaner as above. Dry clean as soon as possible.

SHOE POLISH **Combination**

These greasy/waxy stains also contain dye and present as black or brown smears.

Removal
Moderate – the stains spread readily, so work from the outside of the stain inwards

Scrape off as much excess polish as possible with a spoon or blunt knife, then rub washing-up liquid into the back of the stain. Place the surface of the stain over scrunched-up kitchen towels or an absorbent white cloth and rub a warm-water detergent solution on to the back of the stain. Repeat as necessary. Launder in the hottest water that is safe for the fabric.

On carpets and upholstery, spray or sponge with soda water, saturating the stained area. Keep blotting and reapplying soda water until the stain has lifted. If the stain persists, apply a weak solution of washing-up liquid and water and blot.

Scrape off excess polish as above, then spot treat with white spirit, blotting at the back of the stain (see page 7). Rinse the solvent thoroughly from the fabric and air dry before laundering.

Another method is to spot treat with grease-solvent stain remover, feathering at the back of the stain. Rinse the solvent thoroughly from the fabric and air dry before laundering.

Alternatively, rub biological (enzyme) liquid detergent into both sides of the stain. Leave this on and launder with biological (enzyme) detergent in the hottest water that is safe for the fabric.

For really stubborn stains, and if the fabric can take it, spot treat with paintbrush cleaning fluid.

SILICONE Greasy

Most commonly found in brake fluid, silicone is also used as a syringe lubricant. It is a slippery, clear, oily substance that does not absorb moisture. Wipe up any spills promptly as silicone spreads rapidly.

Removal
Moderate

 Blot up as much excess fluid as possible with kitchen towels or an absorbent white cloth. Sprinkle the stain with bicarbonate of soda, cornflour or talcum powder and rub in gently. Leave for 30 minutes, then wipe off with a dry flannel facecloth. This method works on both washable and non-washable fabrics.

Alternatively, work a little washing-up liquid into both sides of the stain. Leave for 5 minutes before soaking in a bucket of water to which ½ cup washing-up liquid has been added. Leave for 30 minutes.

If the stain persists, mix bicarbonate of soda with a little cold water to make a thick paste, apply and leave until it has dried completely, then brush off.

Launder in the hottest water that is safe for the fabric in a 50/50 detergent/bicarbonate of soda wash.

On carpets and upholstery, blot up and sprinkle with powder as above. Leave overnight, then vacuum. If the stain persists, squirt over a tiny amount of shaving cream and brush gently into the fibres with an old toothbrush. Wipe away excess foam with a clean dry cloth and blot with a sponge dipped in cold water.

 Blot up and sprinkle with powder as above, then spot treat with grease-solvent stain remover, feathering at the back of the stain (see page 7). Rinse thoroughly from the fabric and air dry before laundering.

Alternatively, rub biological (enzyme) liquid detergent into both sides, then launder with biological (enzyme) detergent in the hottest water that is safe for the fabric.

SOFT DRINKS Tannin

Non-alcoholic carbonated drinks full of food colourings cause a variety of coloured stains, from cola-brown to cherry-pink.

 Rinse immediately in cold water. Rub washing-up liquid into the back of the stain and gently agitate the back of the fabric against itself. Rinse and launder.

If the stain has dried in, apply glycerine to the back, then leave for 30 minutes before treating as above.

On non-washable fabrics, sponge with cold water, then spot treat with methylated spirits (see page 7). Rinse and launder.

Removal
Moderate

Make sure every trace of spill is removed as quickly as possible. Some stains containing sugar will be invisible when they dry but turn yellow with heat or age, and will be impossible to remove.

DON'T use any kind of soap – soap sets soft drinks stains.

 Rinse immediately in cold water. Rub biological (enzyme) liquid detergent into the back of the stain and gently agitate the back of the fabric against itself. Launder with biological (enzyme) detergent in the hottest water that is safe for the fabric.

   If the stain persists, apply stain stick to both sides of the stain and launder again.

   On carpets and upholstery, blot up as much excess liquid as possible with kitchen towels or an absorbent cloth. Dilute biological (enzyme) liquid detergent in cold water and agitate to froth it up. Sponge over the area, then sponge off with cold water. Repeat until as much of the stain as possible has been removed. If the stain persists, treat with carpet stain remover.

SOOT/SMOKE Special

Soot is made up of the powdery, dust-like, black carbon particles that are formed by combustion. Smoke stains consist of the same substances, but the particles are much finer.

Removal
Moderate

 Take the fabric outside and shake out as much excess dust as possible. Carefully vacuum the stained area, taking care not to spread the mark even further. Sprinkle the stain with bicarbonate of soda, salt or talcum powder and leave for 5 minutes, then vacuum again. Repeat as necessary.

   On carpets and upholstery, vacuum up as much excess dust as possible. Sprinkle the stain with salt and leave for several hours, then vacuum. Repeat as necessary. On pale-coloured carpets, use Fuller's earth instead of salt.

 Shake and vacuum off excess dust as above. Sponge a warm-water solution of biological (enzyme) detergent on to the back of the stain, then rinse in cool water.

   Alternatively, spot treat with dry-cleaning solvent, dabbing at the back of the stain (see page 7). Rinse the solvent thoroughly from the fabric and air dry before laundering.

   Apply a paste of powdered biological (enzyme) detergent and warm water to both sides and launder in the hottest water that is safe for the fabric.

   Non-washable fabrics can be treated with spot dry-cleaning solvent, but it is safer to take them to the dry cleaner as soon as possible.

SOUP Combination

These stains can be any colour, from brown chicken soup through green to red tomato soup, and are best identified by smell.

Removal
Moderate – tomato soup requires some work because of its high acid content

 Dilute 2 cups white vinegar in a bowl of warm water, colour test and leave to soak for 2 hours.

Rub non-bleach liquid detergent into both sides of the stain and leave for 1 hour. Launder.

If the stain persists, spot treat with methylated spirits (see page 7). Rinse and launder.

 Dampen the stain with cool water and rub stain stick on to both sides of the stain. Launder with biological (enzyme) detergent in the hottest water that is safe for the fabric.

You can also use red-wine solvent stain remover on tomato soup stains.

If the stain persists, soak the fabric in all-fabric bleach solution for 15 minutes, rinse and then launder. If the stain still remains, and the fabric can take it, soak in chlorine bleach solution for 15 minutes, rinse and launder.

Spot treat tough stains with dry-cleaning solvent, blotting at the back of the stain. Rinse thoroughly from the fabric and air dry before laundering.

SOY SAUCE Tannin

This sauce is a combination of roasted barley or wheat and fermented soya beans and leaves light or dark brown stains.

Removal
Easy to moderate

DON'T use soap of any kind – soap sets soy sauce stains.

 Hold the back of the stain under the full force of a running cold tap.

Rub liquid detergent into both sides of the stain and leave to soak in warm water for 30 minutes, gently agitating the back of the fabric against itself from time to time.

If soy sauce spills on a white tablecloth over a meal, soak a piece of bread in soda water and use as a sponge, leaving it to cover the stain until it can be cleaned. If none is to hand, use cold water.

On carpets and upholstery, dilute liquid detergent in warm water and agitate to froth it up. Blot the stain, then blot with clear warm water. Repeat as necessary. If the stain persists, dilute 1 tablespoon ammonia in ½ cup water and colour test. Blot the stain alternately with the ammonia solution and clean water as before.

Soak in a biological (enzyme) pre-soak for 30 minutes. Apply liquid biological (enzyme) detergent to both sides. Launder in the hottest water that is safe.

If the stain persists, soak in all-fabric bleach solution for 15 minutes, rinse and launder. If the stain still remains, and the fabric can take it, soak in chlorine bleach solution for 15 minutes, rinse and launder.

SUNTAN OIL/LOTION OR SUNBLOCK *Greasy*

Made with oils designed to penetrate the skin, these lotions create clear, greasy stains that are often denser in the centre than at the edge.

Removal
Moderate

Scrape off as much excess lotion as possible with a spoon or an old credit card, working from the outside of the stain inwards to avoid spreading it any further. Sprinkle with bicarbonate of soda, cornflour or talcum powder and rub gently into the stain. Leave for 30 minutes to allow the powder to absorb the lotion, then wipe off with a dry flannel facecloth. This method works on both washable and non-washable fabrics.

Alternatively, work a little washing-up liquid into both sides. Leave for 5 minutes before soaking in a bucket of water to which ½ cup washing-up liquid has been added. Leave for 30 minutes.

On carpets and upholstery, scrape off and sprinkle with powder as above to absorb the excess lotion. Leave for several hours – overnight if possible – then vacuum. If the stain persists, squirt a tiny amount of shaving cream over the stain and brush gently into the fibres with an old toothbrush. Wipe away excess foam with a clean dry cloth and blot with a sponge dipped in cold water.

 Scrape off excess lotion as above, then spot treat with grease-solvent stain remover, feathering at the back of the stain (see page 7). Rinse the solvent thoroughly from the fabric and air dry before laundering.

Alternatively, rub biological (enzyme) liquid detergent into both sides of the stain. Leave this on and launder with biological (enzyme) detergent in the hottest water that is safe for the fabric.

SWEETS Tannin

Combinations of sugar and food colourings cause a variety of coloured stains, from cola-brown to cherry-pink.

Removal
Moderate

Make sure every trace of the sweet is removed as quickly as possible. Some stains containing sugar will be invisible when they dry but turn yellow with heat or age, and these stains will be impossible to remove.

DON'T use soap of any kind – soap sets sweet stains.

 Wipe off any sticky mess with a hot, damp flannel facecloth, then rinse immediately in cold water. Rub washing-up liquid into the back of the stain and gently agitate the fabric against itself. Rinse and launder.

If the stain has dried in, apply glycerine to the back and leave for 30 minutes before treating as above. On non-washable fabrics, sponge with cold water and then spot treat with methylated spirits (see page 7).

 Wipe and rinse as above. Rub biological (enzyme) liquid detergent into the back and gently agitate the fabric against itself. Launder with biological (enzyme) detergent in the hottest water that is safe for the fabric.

If the stain persists, apply stain stick to both sides of the fabric and launder again.

On carpets and upholstery, wipe and rinse as above. Dilute biological (enzyme) liquid detergent in cold water and froth up. Sponge on, then sponge off with cold water. Treat any traces with carpet stain remover.

SYRUP Tannin

Syrup leaves a yellowish, sticky stain.

Removal
Moderate

Make sure every trace of a spill is removed as quickly as possible. Some stains containing sugar will be invisible when they dry but turn yellow with heat or age, and these will be impossible to remove.

DON'T use soap of any kind – soap sets syrup stains.

 Scrape off as much syrup as possible with a spoon or blunt knife, then rinse immediately in cold water. Rub washing-up liquid into the back and gently agitate the back of the fabric against itself. Rinse and launder.

If the stain has dried in, apply glycerine to the back and leave for 30 minutes before treating as above.

On non-washable fabrics, sponge with cold water, then spot treat with methylated spirits (see page 7).

 Rinse immediately in cold water. Rub biological (enzyme) liquid detergent into the back and gently agitate the back of the fabric against itself, then launder with biological (enzyme) detergent. If it persists, apply stain stick to both sides. Launder.

On carpets and upholstery, blot up excess syrup with kitchen towels or an absorbent cloth. Dilute biological (enzyme) liquid detergent in cold water and agitate to froth it up. Sponge on, then sponge off with cold water.

TAR Dye

Tar is a black or grey sticky substance that can be trodden into carpets unsuspectingly or get on to clothing.

Removal
Difficult

 On clothing, harden in the freezer for 30 minutes or so. Scrape and pick off as much tar as you can with your fingernails and a blunt knife, being careful not to damage the fibres.

Spot treat with glycerine, tapping at the back of the stain with an old toothbrush or spoon (see page 7). If the stain has dried in, warm the glycerine a little before applying.

Rub turpentine or eucalyptus oil into the back of the remaining mark and keep blotting.

If the stain persists, apply liquid detergent to the back of the stain and gently agitate the back of the fabric against itself in hot water. Launder in the hottest water that is safe for the fabric.

On carpets or upholstery, blot up as much tar as possible with kitchen towels, then sponge with turpentine or eucalyptus oil. Apply a soapy detergent solution, scrubbing gently with an old toothbrush or nailbrush, and rinse.

 Freeze and scrape as above, then spot treat with dye-solvent stain remover on the back. Rinse thoroughly from the fabric and air dry, then launder. If the stain persists, rub in biological (enzyme) liquid detergent. Leave this on and launder with biological (enzyme) detergent in the hottest water that is safe for the fabric.

TARNISH Organic

Discoloration on metals caused by oxidization creates black stains that transfer readily to other surfaces.

Removal
Easy

 On tarnished pots and pans, cover with tomato ketchup and leave for 5 minutes. Wipe off.

On fabrics, spot treat with white vinegar (colour test first) or lemon juice, blotting at the back of the stain (see page 7). Rinse and launder.

 Colour test and then spot treat with 3 per cent hydrogen peroxide bleach (NOT hair bleach, see page 16), blotting at the back of the stain. Rinse the solvent thoroughly from the fabric and air dry, then launder as usual.

TEA **Tannin**

Tea leaves brown stains.

Removal
Easy

DON'T use soap of any kind –
soap sets tea stains.

 Mix a paste from bicarbonate of soda and a little water and spread on to the stain. Leave for 15 minutes and rinse. Repeat as necessary.

On porcelain and white steel sinks and surfaces, cover with bicarbonate of soda paste and leave for 15 minutes. Scour and rinse.

On carpets and upholstery, spray or sponge with soda water, saturating the area. Keep blotting and reapplying until the stain has lifted. If the stain persists, apply a weak solution of washing-up liquid and water to the stain and blot. Repeat as necessary.

 On both washable and non-washable fabrics, sponge the back of the stain with a solution of 1 tablespoon biological (enzyme) liquid detergent in 1 cup warm water. Rinse.

If the stain persists, soak washable fabrics in biological (enzyme) pre-soak for 30 minutes. Launder with biological (enzyme) detergent in the hottest water that is safe for the fabric. Take non-washable fabrics to the dry cleaner as soon as possible.

TOBACCO **Special**

Tobacco leaves pale brown stains.

Removal
Moderate

 Loosen old stains by rubbing glycerine into both sides and leave for 30 minutes before treatment.

Mix 1 tablespoon white vinegar in 1 litre (2 pints) warm water and add a squirt of washing-up liquid. Colour test, then leave to soak for 30 minutes. Rinse and air dry.

If the stain persists, spot treat with methylated spirits (see page 7). Rinse and launder.

Treat carpets and upholstery with methylated spirits, then use an absorbent white cloth to dab meths over the stain, rubbing gently. Rinse. Repeat as necessary. If the stain persists, squirt a tiny amount of shaving cream over the stain and brush gently into the fibres with an old toothbrush. Wipe away the excess foam with a clean dry cloth and blot with a sponge dipped in cold water.

Rub cigarette burns on furniture with fine steel wool, then rub in linseed oil or methylated spirits.

 Spray with a spot-treatment stain remover for tobacco stains. Leave for 30 minutes, then launder.

Alternatively, dampen the stain with cold water and rub stain stick on to both sides. Launder.

If you do not have either treatments to hand, make a paste from powdered biological (enzyme) detergent and water. Apply to both sides of the stain before laundering as usual.

Take non-washable fabrics to the dry cleaner as soon as possible.

TOMATO JUICE Tannin

These thick, red liquid stains can be identified by smell.

Removal
Moderate

DON'T use soap of any kind – soap sets tomato juice stains.

 Scrape off as much excess juice as possible with a spoon or an old credit card and rinse immediately under cold running water, gently agitating the back of the fabric against itself and letting the water run through. Colour test and then dab white vinegar all over the back of the stain. Rinse through again. Repeat several times. Launder.

Rub glycerine into the back of the stain and leave to soak in warm, soapy water for 1 hour. Rinse and launder as usual.

 Scrape off excess juice and rinse as above. Apply biological (enzyme) liquid detergent to both sides of the stain and launder in the hottest water that is safe for the fabric.

Alternatively, colour test, then spot treat with red-wine stain remover, dabbing at the back of the stain (see page 7). Rinse the solvent thoroughly from the fabric and air dry before laundering. If traces of the stain remain, rub in biological (enzyme) liquid detergent. Leave this on and launder with biological (enzyme) detergent in the hottest water that is safe for the fabric.

If the stain persists, soak in all-fabric bleach solution for 15 minutes, rinse and launder. If the stain still remains, and the fabric can take it, soak in chlorine bleach solution for 15 minutes, rinse and launder.

TOMATO SAUCE **Combination**

These red stains are often mistaken for blood.

Removal
Moderate – easy if the stain hasn't set

 Scrape off as much excess sauce as possible with a spoon or an old credit card and rinse immediately under cold running water, gently agitating the back of the fabric against itself and letting the water run through. Colour test, then dab white vinegar all over the back of the stain, then rinse through again. Repeat several times. Launder.

Work liquid detergent into the back of the stain and launder in the hottest water that is safe for the fabric.

Alternatively, rub glycerine into the back of the stain and leave to soak in warm, soapy water for 1 hour. Rinse and launder.

 Scrape off excess sauce and rinse as above. Apply biological (enzyme) liquid detergent to both sides of the stain and launder in the hottest water that is safe for the fabric.

Alternatively, colour test and then spot treat with red-wine stain remover, dabbing at the back of the stain (see page 7). Rinse the solvent thoroughly from the fabric and air dry before laundering. If traces of the stain remain, rub in biological (enzyme) liquid detergent. Leave this on and launder with biological (enzyme) detergent in the hottest water that is safe for the fabric.

If the stain persists, soak in all-fabric bleach solution for 15 minutes, rinse and launder. If the stain still remains, and the fabric can take it, soak in chlorine bleach solution for 15 minutes, rinse and launder.

TOOTHPASTE Tannin

The white or blue marks left by toothpaste can be identified by the minty smell.

Removal
Easy

DON'T use soap of any kind – soap sets toothpaste stains.

 Scrape off as much excess toothpaste as possible with a spoon or blunt knife.

Mix 1 tablespoon white vinegar in 1 litre (2 pints) warm water. Add a squirt of washing-up liquid. Colour test, then soak for 30 minutes. Rinse and air dry.

 Soak in a biological (enzyme) pre-soak for 30 minutes or make a paste from powdered biological (enzyme) detergent and water, apply to both sides, then launder in the hottest water that is safe for the fabric.

UNKNOWN STAINS Various

Look for clues, such as smells. Grease stains will often fade towards the edges; old grease stains may have a rancid smell but look like dry stains. Colour is not always a good guide: for example, rust-coloured stains could be the caramelized sugar from lemonade or caused by the benzoyl peroxide bleach in some cosmetics. Always handle unknown red stains with care – wear rubber gloves in case they are blood.

Removal
Easy to impossible

 Keep in mind the two big don'ts: don't use soap, and don't use hot water. Soap sets tannin stains; hot water sets protein stains.

Rinse in cool water. Apply washing-up liquid to both sides and gently agitate the back of the fabric against itself. Rinse in cool water. Repeat several times.

Alternatively, soak for 30 minutes in liquid detergent and cold water.

If the stain persists, on all fabrics except cottons and linens, dilute 1 teaspoon white vinegar in 1 cup cool water. Colour test and apply to the back of the stain with an absorbent white cloth, rubbing gently.

If the stain still remains, and for cottons and linens, dilute equal parts methylated spirits with cool water and apply as above.

If traces of the stain remain, dissolve 1 teaspoon ammonia in 1 cup cool water and apply again.

 If the stain looks waxy and heavy, sponge with dry-cleaning solvent. Air dry.

Alternatively, make a paste from biological (enzyme) detergent and cool water, apply to both sides of the stain and launder at a low temperature.

If the stain persists, soak in all-fabric bleach solution for 15 minutes, rinse and launder. If the stain still remains, and the fabric can take it, soak in chlorine bleach solution for 15 minutes, rinse and launder.

URINE Protein

Urine stains are a dull yellow with an unmistakeable acidic smell.

Removal
Easy – moderate if dried in

 Rinse under cold running water and launder. If the stain has set, soak for 1 hour in borax first. Colour test and dab small spots with white vinegar or tea tree oil.

For pet and baby urine on carpets, mattresses and furniture, sponge up residue. Rub in a 50/50 mixture of white vinegar and warm soapy water. Leave to dry.

 Rinse under cold running water. Soak overnight in biological (enzyme) detergent, then launder. If the stain is old and stubborn, soak in cold water for 1 hour, then apply biological (enzyme) pre-soak and launder.

If the stain persists, soak in all-fabric bleach solution for 15 minutes, rinse and launder. If the stain still remains, and the fabric can take it, soak in chlorine bleach solution for 15 minutes, rinse and launder.

If the area has changed colour after all this, dab the area with a solution of 1 teaspoon ammonia in 1 cup water, rinse and launder. On non-washable fabrics, alternate between sponging with warm biological (enzyme) detergent solution and cold water.

Do the same with carpets, furniture and mattresses – add a few drops of disinfectant to the water. When the stain has gone, rinse, wash with carpet or upholstery shampoo and air dry. If it has changed colour, treat with ammonia as above. If a smell lingers, sprinkle with calcium carbonate, leave for 24 hours and vacuum.

VARNISH Special

Craft or wood varnish stains are transparent, drying to a clear, hard finish. Nail varnish will do the same but could be any colour.

Removal
Moderate

 On all fabrics except acetate, spot treat as soon as possible with methylated spirits (see page 7).

Use this treatment on carpets and upholstery. If the stain persists, squirt a tiny amount of shaving cream over the stain and brush gently into the fibres with an old toothbrush. Wipe away excess foam with a clean dry cloth and blot with a sponge dipped in cold water.

 For all fabrics except acetate, spot treat with a non-greasy nail varnish remover. Repeat with carpets and upholstery. Use carpet stain remover on any residue.

VEGETABLE OIL *Greasy*

This non-toxic clear oil causes yellowish stains.

Removal
Moderate

 Dab up as much excess oil as possible with kitchen towels or an absorbent white cloth, then sprinkle with bicarbonate of soda, cornflour or talcum powder and rub gently into the stain. Leave for 30 minutes to allow the powder to absorb the oil, then wipe off with a dry flannel facecloth. This method works on both washable and non-washable fabrics.

Alternatively, work a little washing-up liquid into both sides of the stain. Leave for 5 minutes before soaking in a bucket of water to which ½ cup washing-up liquid has been added. Leave for 30 minutes.

Launder in the hottest water that is safe for the fabric in a 50/50 detergent/bicarbonate of soda wash.

On carpets and upholstery, dab up and sprinkle with powder to absorb excess oil as above. Leave for several hours – overnight if possible – then vacuum. If the stain persists, squirt a tiny amount of shaving cream over the stain and brush gently into the fibres with an old toothbrush. Wipe away excess foam with a clean dry cloth and blot with a sponge dipped in cold water.

 Dab off and sprinkle with powder as above to absorb excess oil, then spot treat with grease-solvent stain remover, feathering at the back of the stain (see page 7). Rinse the solvent thoroughly from the fabric and air dry before laundering.

Alternatively, rub biological (enzyme) liquid detergent into both sides of the stain. Leave this on and launder with biological (enzyme) detergent in the hottest water that is safe for the fabric.

VOMIT **Protein**

Vomit usually leaves pale brown stains. If in doubt, you can identify by smell.

Removal
Easy

DON'T use hot water, tumble dry or iron until the stain has been removed completely – heat sets vomit stains.

 Clear up as much excess vomit as possible with kitchen towels. Rinse immediately under cold running water or soak in cold water, gently agitating the back of the fabric against itself.

Bleach whites and baby clothes with lemon juice and leave in the sun to dry.

On carpets and upholstery, clear up excess vomit as above. Spray or sponge with soda water to saturate. Keep blotting and reapplying until the stain has lifted. If it doesn't all come out, squirt over a tiny amount of shaving cream and brush gently into the fibres with an old toothbrush. Wipe away excess foam with a clean dry cloth and blot with a sponge dipped in cold water.

On non-washable fabrics, dilute 1 teaspoon ammonia in 1 cup lukewarm water, colour test and sponge over. If it persists, dry clean as soon as possible.

 Clear up excess vomit as above. Gently agitate the back of the fabric against itself in cold water with biological (enzyme) detergent or pre-soak, then leave to soak overnight. If the stain persists, cover both sides of the stain with biological (enzyme) liquid detergent or stain stick and launder in warm water.

On carpets and upholstery, clean up excess as above. Make a solution from warm water, biological (enzyme) detergent and a little disinfectant, and sponge over. Treat any traces with soda water as above. Add a few drops of antiseptic to the final rinse. Treat with a pet stain and odour remover if the smell persists.

WATER SPOTS **Special**

Minerals in water transferred on to fabric cause white spotting, occurring most frequently on rayon, silk and fine wool.

 Try scratching lightly with the point of a sharp knife.

For all fabrics except chiffon and silk, hold over a steaming kettle. Cover the spout with cheesecloth or a clean dishcloth to prevent splashes. Wearing oven gloves, hold the edges well away from the spout. Once steam has penetrated, take away. Using an absorbent white cloth, gently rub the mark from the outside edge inwards with the back of a spoon. Iron while damp.

Removal

Difficult – some water-spot marks are water soluble and will never come out

 On non-washable fabrics, blot with kitchen towels or an absorbent white cloth. Dry clean as soon as possible.

Carpets and upholstery should be professionally treated. If not transportable, cover the stain with kitchen towels or an absorbent white cloth to absorb moisture and weigh down with a pile of books. Dry out with a hairdryer or fan, replacing the towels or cloth as the water is absorbed into it.

WAX Greasy

These stains result from candle, furniture and modelling waxes. They are usually found in clusters of solid, cloudy circles – the hard bits of wax are easy to scrape off, but an oily stain may remain and is more difficult to remove.

Removal
Moderate

 Cover with ice cubes or put in the freezer for a few minutes to harden. Crack the surface and gently scrape with a blunt knife, then pick at the remaining bits with your fingernail. Place the fabric between kitchen towels and press the back with a warm iron. Keep moving the paper around as the wax is absorbed.

This process may force part of the stain into the fibres, leaving an oily-looking residue. If this happens, dab with methylated spirits. For nylon, dilute the meths 50/50 with water first. Rinse and launder.

On carpets and upholstery, chill with ice, then pick out as much wax as you can with a knife and your fingernails as above. Cover the wax with a towel or several layers of kitchen towel and apply a warm iron. Rub with methylated spirits before shampooing.

For tables, pick off the hard bits of wax. Wash with a solution of 1 part white vinegar to 2 parts hot water.

 Harden and scrape off excess wax as above. Apply an aerosol pre-treatment spray and scrub by hand with biological (enzyme) liquid detergent in very hot water.

If you use the ironing method above and are left with an oily spot, treat with spot stain remover before laundering in the hottest water that is safe for the fabric. If the stain persists, bleach with the strongest bleach solution that is safe for the fabric.

Treat non-washable fabrics with dry-cleaning solvent.

Spot treat furniture with grease-solvent stain remover, dabbing at the back (see page 7). Rinse thoroughly and air dry, then launder. If the stain persists, rub biological (enzyme) liquid detergent into both sides, then launder with biological (enzyme) detergent.

WINE, RED Tannin

These pink to deep red marks often appear on tablecloths and tables as ring marks.

Removal
Moderate

DON'T use soap of any kind – soap sets red-wine stains.

 Treat immediately. Saturate the stain with soda water, white wine or cold water and blot with kitchen towels or an absorbent white cloth. Cover the stain with salt and leave for 5 minutes, then rinse in cold water, gently agitating the back of fabric against itself. Repeat as necessary.

On carpets and upholstery, treat with soda water, wine or water and salt as above. Make a paste from 3 parts borax or bicarbonate of soda to 1 part warm water. Apply and leave to dry, then vacuum off.

 Red-wine stain removers are very effective; they also work well on tomato-based stains. Apply as directed.

Alternatively, rinse, blot and cover with salt as above, then rub liquid biological (enzyme) detergent into the back. Leave for 5 minutes and rinse in cold water. Launder with biological (enzyme) detergent.

If the stain is persists, soak the fabric in all-fabric bleach solution for 15 minutes, rinse and launder. If the stain still remains, and the fabric can take it, soak in chlorine bleach solution for 15 minutes, then rinse and launder.

Bleach out old red-wine marks on unvarnished wood using wood bleach applied with a dropper. Polish up with a little shoe polish to restore the colour.

WINE, WHITE Tannin

These dark to pale yellowish stains often appear on tablecloths and tables as ring marks. If in doubt, smell.

Removal
Moderate

DON'T use soap of any kind – soap sets white wine stains.

 Treat immediately. Saturate the stain with soda water or cold water and blot with kitchen towels or an absorbent white cloth. Cover the stain with salt and leave for 5 minutes, then rinse in cold water, gently agitating the back of the fabric against itself. Repeat as necessary with more soda water or water and salt, then rinse.

If the stain persists, work washing-up liquid into both sides of the stain and rinse.

If the stain still remains, make a paste from 3 parts borax or bicarbonate of soda to 1 part warm water. Apply to the stain and leave to dry, then brush off.

On carpets and upholstery, treat with soda water or water and salt as before. Then make a paste from 3 parts borax or bicarbonate of soda to 1 part warm water. Apply to the stain and leave to dry, then vacuum off.

 Rinse, blot and cover with salt as before, then rub biological (enzyme) liquid detergent into the back of the stain. Leave for 5 minutes and rinse in cold water. Launder with biological (enzyme) detergent.

Alternatively, spray with general-purpose pre-laundry spot stain remover, leave for 5 minutes and launder with biological enzyme detergent.

WOOD SAP **Combination**

Wood sap is a watery, sticky sap containing sugar, salt and minerals that in the home issues from Christmas trees, pine cones and any soft wooden surface warmed by sunlight or other heat.

Removal
Moderate

 Scrape off as much excess sap as possible with a spoon or blunt knife, then spot treat with glycerine, tapping at the back of the stain with an old toothbrush or spoon (see page 7). If the stain has dried in, warm the glycerine a little before applying. Then rub washing-up liquid into the back of the stain and rinse under cool running water, gently agitating the back of the fabric against itself.

If the stain persists, spot treat with turpentine.

 Apply resin or sap stain remover to both sides of the stain and leave for 10 minutes or as directed. If the stain persists, rub biological (enzyme) liquid detergent into both sides of the stain. Leave this on and launder with biological (enzyme) detergent in the hottest water that is safe for the fabric.

For old, tough stains, spot treat with dry-cleaning solvent. Rinse thoroughly from the fabric and air dry before laundering with biological (enzyme) detergent.

If any colour still remains, treat as a dye stain (see page 57).

Take non-washable fabrics to the dry cleaner as soon as possible.

YELLOWING Special

These stains can appear on whites that have gone off-colour after storage. Yellowing caused by over-bleaching is permanent.

Removal
Moderate

 Make a solution of 1 part white vinegar to 12 parts cool water, colour test and then soak overnight. Rinse and launder.

Alternatively, dissolve 2–3 denture cleaning tablets in a bowl of warm water and soak for several hours.

 Leave to soak in net curtain whitener as directed.

YOGURT Protein

These stains come in a variety of colours and consistencies, and are easily identified by smell.

Removal
Easy

DON'T use hot water, tumble dry or iron until the stain has been removed completely – heat sets yogurt stains.

 Scrape off as much excess yogurt as possible with a spoon. Spot treat the back of the stain with soda water or soak the fabric immediately in cold water. Gently agitate the back of the fabric against itself or hold the back of the stain under cold running water and let it run through for 5 minutes or until the stain disappears.

On carpets and upholstery, spray or sponge with soda water, saturating the area. Keep blotting and reapplying soda water until the stain has lifted.

If the stain persists, squirt a tiny amount of shaving cream over the stain and brush gently into the fibres with an old toothbrush. Wipe away excess foam with a dry cloth and blot with a damp sponge.

 Scrape off excess yogurt as above. Dampen with cool water, then apply stain stick to both sides of the stain. Launder with biological (enzyme) detergent in warm water as usual.

If the stain persists, rub biological (enzyme) liquid detergent on to both sides of the stain on dry fabric. Alternatively, make a paste from biological (enzyme) detergent and warm water and rub on to both sides of wet fabric. Rinse and launder as above.

On non-washable fabrics, dab with lukewarm water and treat with dry-cleaning spot remover.

For old, stubborn stains, rub biological (enzyme) detergent into the stain as above and leave to soak in cool water for 4 hours, gently agitating the back of the fabric against itself from time to time.

INDEX

For individual stains see A–Z list.

M

mattresses, 10
meat tenderizer, 13
methylated spirits, 10
milk, 13
mohair, 22

N

nail varnish remover, 7,
    17
net, 22
nylon, 22

O

onions, 13
organic stains, 5
oxygen bleach, 16

P

paint remover, 17
petroleum-based solvents, 7
pillows, 10
polyester, 22
potatoes, 13
pre-treatment products, 17
protein stains, 3
pumice stone, 13–14

R

rayon, 22
red-wine solvent stain
remover, 10
rottenstone, 14
rubbing alcohol, 7, 11
rust removers, 7, 17

S

safety, chemicals, 8
salt, 10, 14
satin, 22
serge, 22
shaving cream, 14
silk, 22–3
soap, 14
soda water, 9, 10, 14
sodium hypochlorite, 16
sodium perborate, 16
special stains, 4, 5
spot remover, 16
spot-treatment techniques, 7
stains: chemical stain-removal
    products, 6–7, 15–17
    natural stain-removal
products, 11–15
    removal techniques, 6–10
    types of stain, 3–5
suede, 23
sugar tannin stains, 4

T

talcum powder, 14
tannin stains, 3–4
tea tree oil, 14
temperature, laundering, 9
tile cleaners, 17
toothpaste, 14
towelling, 23
triacetate, 19
trisodium phosphate (TSP), 17
turpentine, 7, 15
tweed, 23

U

unknown stains, 4, 5
upholstery, 7, 9–10

V

varnish remover, 17
velour, 23
velvet, 23
vinegar, white, 10, 15
viscose rayon, 22
viyella, 23

W

warning labels, 8
washing, 8–9
washing soda, 10, 15
washing-up liquid, 15
white spirit, 17
white vinegar, 10, 15
whitener, 16
wool, 23

ACKNOWLEDGEMENTS

Executive Editor
Sarah Tomley
Editor
Charlotte Wilson
Executive Art Editor
Karen Sawyer
Design and illustration
'ome Design
Production Controller
Manjit Sihra